Helion & Company Limited
Unit 8 Amherst Business Centre
Budbrooke Road
Warwick
CV34 5WE
England
Tel. 01926 499 619
Email: info@helion.co.uk
Website: www.helion.co.uk
Twitter: @helionbooks
Visit our blog http://blog.helion.co.uk/

Text © David Francois 2021
Photographs © as individually credited
Colour artworks ©Renato Dalmaso, Luca Canossa and Tom Cooper 2021
Maps © Tom Cooper 2021

Designed and typeset by Farr out Publications, Wokingham, Berkshire
Cover design Paul Hewitt, Battlefield Design (www.battlefield-design.co.uk)

Every reasonable effort has been made to trace copyright holders and to obtain their permission for the use of copyright material. The author and publisher apologise for any errors or omissions in this work, and would be grateful if notified of any corrections that should be incorporated in future reprints or editions of this book.

ISBN 978-1-914377-07-5

British Library Cataloguing-in-Publication Data
A catalogue record for this book is available from the British Library

All rights reserved. No part of this publication may be reproduced, stored in a retrieval system, or transmitted, in any form, or by any means, electronic, mechanical, photocopying, recording or otherwise, without the express written consent of Helion & Company Limited.

We always welcome receiving book proposals from prospective authors.

CONTENTS

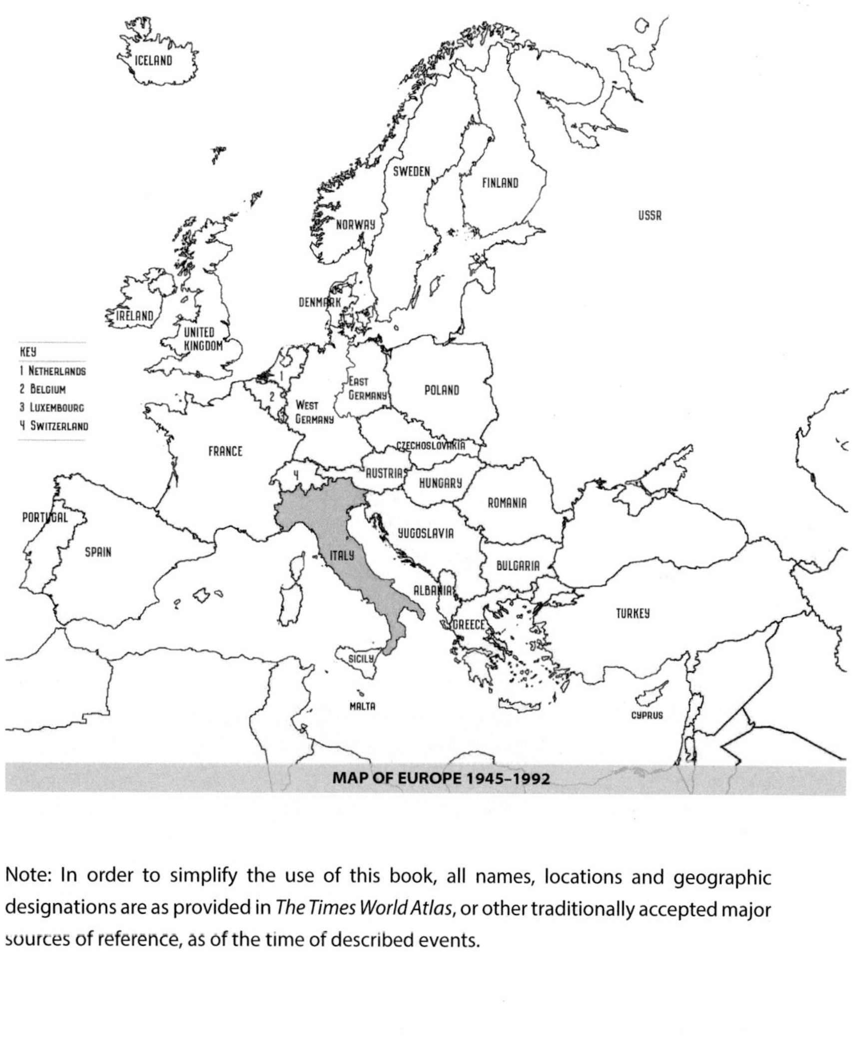

MAP OF EUROPE 1945–1992

Note: In order to simplify the use of this book, all names, locations and geographic designations are as provided in *The Times World Atlas*, or other traditionally accepted major sources of reference, as of the time of described events.

ABBREVIATIONS

AO	*Avanguardia Operaia* (Worker Vanguard)
BR	*Brigate Rosse* (Red Brigades)
BR-PCC	*Brigate Rosse-Partito Comunista Combattente* (Red Brigades-Communist Combatant Party)
BR-PG	*Brigate Rosse-Partito Guerriglia* (Red Brigades-Guerrilla Party)
BR-UCC	*Brigate Rosse-Unione dei Comunisti Combattenti* (Red Brigades-Union of Combatant Communists)
CGIL	*Confederazione Generale Italiana del Lavoro* (Italian General Confederation of Labour)
CISL	*Confederazione Italiana Sindacati dei Lavoratori* (Italian Confederation of Trade Unions)
CISNAL	*Confederazione Italiana Sindacati Nazionali dei Lavoratori* (Italian Confederation of National Trade Unions)
CIA	Central Intelligence Agency [USA]
CLN	*Comitato di Liberazione Nazionale* (National Liberation Committee)
CPM	*Collettivo Politico Metropolitano* (Metropolitan Political Collective)
CPSU	Communist Party of the Soviet Union
CUB	*Comitati Unitari di Base* (Basic Units Committees)
CE	*Comitato Esecutivo* (Executive Committee)
DC	*Democrazia Cristiana* (Christian Democracy)
DIGOS	*Divizione Investigazioni Generali ed Operazioni Speciali* (General Investigations and Special Operations Division)
DS	*Direzione Strategica* (Strategic Direction)
GAP	*Gruppi d'Azione Partigiana* (Partisan Action Groups)
GIS	*Gruppo d'Intervento Speciale* (Special Intervention Group)
GP	*Gauche prolétarienne* (Proletarian Left)[France]
KGB	*Komitet gossoudarstvennoï bezopasnosti* (Committee for State Security)[of the USSR]
LC	*Lotta Continua* (Continuous Struggle)
MSI	*Movimento Sociale Italiano* (Italian Social Movement)
NAP	*Nuclei Armati Proletari* (Armed Proletarian Cells)
NOCS	*Nucleo Operativo Centrale di Sicurezza* (Central Security Task Group)
NSA	*Nucleo Speciale Antiterrorismo* (Special Counterterrorism Unit)
PCI	*Partito Comunista Italiano* (Italian Communist Party)
Pot Op	*Potere Operaio* (Workers Power)
PSI	*Partito Socialista Italiano* (Italian Socialist Party)
PL	*Prima Linea* (Front Line)
RAF	*Rote Armee Fraktion* (Red Army Faction)[FDR]
SID	*Servizio Informazioni Difesa* (Defence Information Service)
SIDA	*Sindacato Italiano dell'Automobile* (Italian Automobile Union)
SIFAR	*Servizio Informazioni Forze Armate* (Armed Forces Information Service)
Stasi	*Ministerium für Staatssicherheit* (Ministry for State Security)[GDR]
StB	*Státní Bezpečnost* (State Security) [Czechoslovakia]
UCIGOS	*Ufficio Centrale per le Investigazioni Generali e per le Operazioni Speciali* (Central office for general investigations and special operations)

INTRODUCTION

The year 1970 in Italy marked the beginning of a period of armed struggle, led by various left-wing groups. A few figures demonstrate a phenomenon that lasted almost two decades; between 1970 and 1982, this 'armed party', as Italian historians and journalists call it, claimed 2,188 attacks, of which 272 were deadly, with 360 people killed or injured.[1] Among the many organisations which formed during this period, it was the *Brigate Rosse* (Red Brigades or BR) which, by their capacity to survive over time, to extend their actions throughout a large part of the country, and to inflict the most severe blows, particularly embodied this moment of armed political violence. They continued their fight, without ceasing, until 1982 and their echoes were still heard in the following decades with a few attacks committed in the 1980s and a sporadic return from 1999 to 2002.

Beyond this longevity, and their central role in the urban Left guerrillas, the BR was distinguished from other groups by the myth that surrounded them. This myth was constructed in the first place by the images created by the media. They were thus described as impenetrable, fierce, relentless, elusive, even incomprehensible, a phenomenon which seemed to be a disturbing and enigmatic spectre of Italian history, and suitable subjects for conspiracy theories. In reality, the BR, although they appeared against a background of growing far-left political violence in much of the Western world, were the fruit of the history of the Italian Left and the strength of the revolutionary myth in this country.[2]

Writing the history of the BR means first of all telling of the defeat of women and men who had chosen to take up arms to give reality to this myth and to take a path considered 'deviant' by the institutional political parties. This is all the more difficult since the history of the BR is tainted with the infamous epithet of 'terrorism'. It is not a question of minimising the seriousness of the responsibilities of the BR's actions compared to people who were neither better, nor especially worse than others, but the term 'terrorist' has become a category in itself, making any reflection unnecessary and depoliticising the authors and actions. We therefore prefer to speak of armed struggle or revolutionary violence, in that it seeks to attack State power following an ideology of radical social change.

The last difficulty in writing the history of the BR is the proliferation over the decades of many conspiratorial theories, at the heart of which lies the idea that the BR were nothing but puppets manipulated by larger forces, whether Italian or foreign. These interpretations, still popular on the editorial level, are especially interesting because they show the difficulty for Italian society in confronting this past, a difficulty all the greater since it is part of a world that has long gone, that of the Cold War. In terms of knowledge, of historical truth, they add nothing. We prefer in this book to rely on the methods of historical science to retrace the trajectory of men and women who practised revolutionary violence at the heart of a Western democracy and made Italy falter. We apologise to the reader eager for sensationalism, but whoever seeks useful knowledge to understand the past and reflect on the present and future world may find some profit in it.

1
COLD WAR IN ITALIA

Italy, like the rest of the Western world, faced at the end of the 1960s a social, political and cultural crisis which expressed the desire for change in society. The political and ruling class was forced to reform the country in order to control the changes underway. This process was not painless in a country whose exit from fascism some 20 years earlier did not lead to a purge and therefore to a significant renewal of the state apparatus; a country which was also at the heart of the challenges of the Cold War having on its territory both American military bases and a powerful communist party. It was in this context that the 1968–1969 protest explosion broke out.

The Fear of Reds

In 1943, after 20 years of fascist rule and following the Allied landings in Sicily and in the south of the peninsula, Italy was divided. Marshal Badoglio and King Victor Emmanuel III took refuge in Brindisi with the Allies after signing the country's surrender in September. In the north, Mussolini created the Italian Social Republic, a puppet state subjugated to Nazi Germany, while in Rome, anti-fascist organisations formed the *Comitato di Liberazione Nazionale* (National Liberation Committee or CLN) which brought together socialists, communists, republicans and Christian democrats. The CLN which, at the end of 1944, controlled 100,000 fighters from partisan brigades, adopted a republican and progressive programme which opposed the King's government, which for its part feared the growing power of the communists.

The situation was resolved in Salerno in March 1944 with the arrival of Palmiro Togliatti, the leader of the *Partito Comunista Italiano* (Italian Communist Party or PCI) who had spent long years in exile in the USSR. Togliatti announced the rallying of the communists to parliamentary democracy resulting in the formation of a new government including CLN members some of whom were communists.[1] The PCI's legalistic orientation was reflected in its integration into the political system in order to guarantee the economic reconstruction of the country within the framework of democracy and respect for the spheres of influence of the great powers, American and Soviet. It also led to the neutralisation of the revolutionary components of the Resistance,

Italian partisans in a firefight on the streets of Milano in May 1945. (Albert Grandolini collection)

Italian partisans that helped liberate Milano in 1945. (Albert Grandolini collection)

Italian police attempting to disperse protesters in 1946. (Albert Grandolini collection)

those partisans who wanted to continue the armed struggle to move from liberation to revolution.[2]

At the end of the war, the National Unity Government began the process of political renewal promised by the CNL. On 6 June 1946, the Italian people voted for the establishment of the Republic and elected a Constituent Assembly. In this election, the *Democrazia Cristiana* (Christian Democracy or DC) obtained 35 percent of the votes, the *Partito Socialista Italiano* (Italian Socialist Party or PSI) 20 percent, and the PCI 19 percent. While Washington was delighted with the success of the DC, it was nonetheless worried about the power of left-wing parties as the Cold War loomed. These fears were justified since the national unity, born during the war, ended when US President Harry Truman proposed the Marshall Plan in 1947, which was rejected by the PCI and the PSI, which turned in opposition to the DC.

Italy was an important strategic stake for the United States, which had been engaged since 12 March 1947 in the policy of containment in the face of Soviet expansionism. The peninsula had a common border with the socialist bloc and formed a crucial lock for the control of the Mediterranean. But Italy also had the most powerful communist party in Western Europe, running the risk that it could fall into the hands of the communists without even the intervention of the Red Army. This situation forced Washington

Election propaganda of 1948. (Albert Grandolini collection)

A DC meeting during the election campaign of 1948. (Albert Grandolini collection)

Togliatti, head of the PCI, during the election campaign of 1948. (Albert Grandolini collection)

to intervene in the country's internal affairs in order to keep it firmly within the Western camp.[3]

The 1948 election campaign saw Italy turn into a real battlefield, a challenge between communism and anti-communism. Despite the ideological and political power of the PCI, several factors made it difficult for it to come to power. First and foremost was the Church, which mobilised the faithful towards openly anti-communist positions. Then there was American support for the DC, organised by the Italian Desk of the Central Intelligence Agency (CIA), headed by James Jesus Angleton. Liberty ships crossed the Atlantic to deliver wheat to the Italians while millions of dollars passed through Vatican banks to finance the DC campaign. Many Italians were thus convinced that only the aid from the United States could enable them to escape poverty and Soviet tyranny. As a precaution, Angleton also sent arms from American military bases in the country to the big cities so that if the Left won, clandestine anti-communist organisations could fight the new power.[4]

If the USSR supported the PCI to finance its electoral campaign, Moscow, faithful to the Yalta accords, accepted that Italy remained in the Western camp. A few days before the elections, Togliatti requested and obtained a meeting with the Soviet ambassador Kostylev. The secret meeting took place near Rome and the Italian leader announced that the PCI leadership was preparing the masses for an armed insurrection. He warned, however, that the latter would only take place in case of extreme necessity, which was to say electoral defeat and, in any case, only after receiving Soviet authorisation. The ambassador's response was clear: 'as regards the seizure of power by armed insurrection, we consider that the PCI is currently in no position to achieve this'.[5] To this curt refusal was added, a few days later, the electoral defeat which saw the DC triumph with 48.5 percent of the vote and the defeat of the Popular Democratic Front, bringing together communists and socialists. Thus disappeared the communist hope of winning power by electoral means.[6]

In order to ward off the threat of the PCI, Washington continued to support the DC as it became the centre of attraction for the middle classes and Catholics and took steps to firmly tie down Italy to the Western camp. In April 1949, the country was among the first signatories of the Atlantic Alliance. The peninsula became Washington's 'aircraft carrier' in the Mediterranean while the Italian armed forces collaborated in setting up the American defence machine. The *Servizio Informazioni Militare* (Military Information Service or SIM), which acted in close cooperation with the CIA, was responsible for combating communist infiltration into administrations, the police and the armed forces. When it became the *Servizio Informazioni Forze Armate* (Armed Forces Information Service or SIFAR[7]) in March 1949, it received from NATO – without informing Parliament – the mission to set up a secret stay-behind network, identical to those organised in the rest of Western Europe. This network, which in Italy took the name of *Gladio*, brought together a few thousand civilian volunteers who learnt, in military bases in Sardinia, the techniques of secret communications, sabotage and guerrilla warfare in order to organise an armed resistance in the event of invasion of the country by Warsaw Pact forces. In addition to this official mission, *Gladio* also appeared as a shadow army

Carlo Sforza, Minister of Foreign Affairs, welcoming General Marshall at the Roma International Airport on 18 October 1948. (Albert Grandolini collection)

intended for clandestine anti-communist operations, especially as it recruited mainly from the former fascists.[8]

Anti-communism brought together both US and Italian ruling circles, the secret services, military officials, stay-behind networks and right-wing extremist forces to prevent Italy from turning to the Left. It also allowed the DC to occupy the leadership of the state from 1948 and made any democratic alternative impossible since its main opponent remained the PCI. This situation of democratic blockage was dangerous and pushed many left-wing activists towards an activism which, for some, led to armed struggle.

Centre-Left Politics

From 1948 on, a 15-year period of exclusive DC rule over Italy began. Its weight in Italian political life and the fear of communism enabled it to draw up a *conventio ad excludendum* (literally 'exclusion agreement') against parties considered dangerous for democracy: the PCI and the PSI above all, but also the *Movimento Sociale Italiano* (Italian Social Movement or MSI), a neo-fascist party founded in 1946 by former representatives of Mussolini's Italian Social Republic.

Alcide De Gasperi, the leader of the DC and President of the Council, firmly linked Italy to the Western bloc and was one of the promoters of European construction: in 1951, Italy was one of the six founding members of the European Coal and Steel Community. In domestic politics, the government was working on the reconstruction of the country by establishing a mixed economy between public and private ownership and by drafting several social laws. However, the DC could not maintain power on its own. It first allied with the Social Democratic Party, born out of a split from the PSI, but, in 1953, when De Gasperi proposed an alliance with the PSI for the municipal elections in Rome, he encountered strong opposition and had to resign.

De Gasperi's successors did not change the political line followed. Thus in 1957, Italy was one of the signatories of the Treaty of Rome, establishing the European Economic Community. At the same time, the general elections continued to demonstrate the DC's political power: 40 percent of the votes in 1953, 42 percent in 1958. However, the PCI grew without interruption and the attempts to form governments composed only of Christian Democrat ministers provoked dissatisfaction from the DC's allies.

Two factions clashed then within the DC. The 'Atlanticists', such as Mario Scelba, Paolo Emilio Taviani and Giulio Andreotti, favourable to an opening on the Right, were opposed to Amintore Fanfani who wanted an alliance with the PSI. At the end of the 1950s, the former prevailed when the MSI became essential for the formation of a political majority led by Fernando Tambroni.[9] This policy was not without risk.

In July 1960, the Tambroni government, supported by the MSI, accepted that this party would hold a congress in Genoa, a city with a strong communist tradition. This decision provoked protests that mobilised students and workers but also former partisans. Left-wing organisations called for a strike on 30 June, which should take place peacefully, but which ended in violent clashes with the police. A solidarity strike soon hit Turin. Faced with this mobilisation, the government banned the holding of the MSI congress, but the demonstrations continued. On 6 July, clashes took place in Rome between the police and the demonstrators and, on 7 July, in Reggio-Emilia, the police shot and killed five workers.[10] On 9 July, the police again shot and killed four workers in Palermo and Catania. The Tambroni government was then forced to resign and was replaced by Fanfani's government.[11]

Political tension resumed in 1962 when, following the announcement of the blockade of Cuba by Washington, PCI's local sections organised a demonstration in Milan that turned into confrontation with the police. One of the demonstrators recounts the level of violence of these confrontations:

> At that time, the police did not have the fancy instruments they have now. Instead of tear gas canisters, they had sorts of boxes, like beer cans, they threw them by rolling them. So, with scarves on their faces for protection from the gas, it was almost a game to pick them up and return them to the sender, as long as they did not burn your hands like the current grenades. The police did not yet have shields, and their batons were much shorter than they are today. They feared physical confrontation because often the workers from Breda or Falck would take to the streets with their helmets and work gloves and it was rough. Even their weaponry was outdated: for rifles they had 91/38s, they used the butt as a baton. But they preferred to charge with the vans. Often, they panicked and they fired shots, which was also why there were so many demonstrators murdered during those years … After the first clashes, the police no longer got out of the vans, because they had already taken a hell of a beating. From the hurrying jeeps,

A car belonging to the communists carrying a model of the Sputnik – the first Soviet satellite shot into the Earth orbit – atop of it, in 1961. (Albert Grandolini collection)

A demonstrator about to attack a jeep of the *Polizia die Stato* (State Police) on the streets of Genoa, in 1960. The primary intervention force of the Corps of Guards of Public Security were the Mobile Units (generically identified as 'Celere' Units): ready-to-use, mobile assets frequently deployed to restore public order during a chaotic period of Italian history, 23 of which were established – one in every major city. (Albert Grandolini collection)

Demonstrations in Genoa during 1960 degenerated in riots that left dozens of police officers wounded, and provoked them into opening fire at the demonstrators. Each of the 20 Mobile Units and the three slightly better equipped and trained Celere Units consisted of three or four mobile companies and one armoured car company. (Albert Grandolini collection)

> some of them held others by their belts, while leaning out of the jeeps and whirling their batons. That way, whoever they managed to nab, they would break their teeth or their head. The counter-attack technique was to take Innocenti tubes [construction tubes for scaffolding] and holding two or three of them, thread them into the driver's cab as the van passed. If the van swerved – and it happened often – we would jump on the occupants and beat them.[12]

The political tensions of the early 1960s did not, however, prevent a displacement of the political majority. The DC's left-wing, led by Aldo Moro, then began to grow and proposed an alliance with the PSI, which in the meantime had broken from the PCI. The socialist leader, Pietro Nenni, was in favour of this option and PSI parliamentarians began, from 1960, to abstain from votes of confidence, the first step towards real collaboration. A compromise between the two parties was found in 1960 with the formation of Fanfani's government allied with the Social Democrats and supported by the Socialists. The presence in this government of Andreotti as Minister of Defence and Scelba as Minister of the Interior was a pledge given to the Atlanticists and to the Americans. In 1962, when Fanfani wanted to form a government that included socialists, the US State Department imposed that the latter did not receive key ministries, so while Andreotti remained Minister of Defence, Taviani received Ministry of the Interior.

In 1963, Moro wanted to go even further in opening up to the Left by forming a government with Nenni as vice-president responsible for implementing a reformist program.[13] He received the agreement of the Pope and that of President Kennedy on the sole condition that Atlanticist ministers were appointed. Moro therefore maintained Andreotti at the Ministry of Defence. But the assassination of President Kennedy was a game-changer. Angleton and the CIA regained control and sounded the alarm, relying on General Giovanni De Lorenzo, Commander-in-Chief of the Carabinieri and former head of SIFAR from 1955 to 1962.

At the top of the Italian State, as in Washington, the opening to the Left was indeed seen as the prelude to a seizure of power by a Marxist movement. SIFAR was then given the mission to infiltrate the PSI to weaken it, and to organise attacks against the DC buildings to fuel a climate of tension and justify emergency measures. In the summer of 1964, the Moro-Nenni government was outvoted. Nenni called for new elections to be held, but the Atlanticists, who feared defeat, sought to avoid this solution. De Lorenzo then prepared the Solo Plan, the objective of which, in the event of disturbances provoked by the Left, was the military occupation of radio and television stations, the closure of left-wing newspapers, and the

Time and again, disruption of public life reached proportions where the Police Celere and Carabinieri had to be reinforced by Italian Army troops. This photograph showing a US-made M8 armoured car and two trucks in support of the Carabinieri was taken in Genoa in 1960. (Albert Grandolini collection)

arrest of more than 700 PCI and PSI leaders.[14] Informed of this plan, Nenni retreated and accepted the formation of a very moderate centre-left government. The Solo Plan showed how the threat of the use of force could constrain a democracy[15].

This threat was all the more concrete as Italy was home to a large far-right, fascinated by the use of force, such as the actions of the Colonels in Greece. This presence of the far-right led to a relatively high level of violence, especially as since 1964 neo-fascist organisations had been in contact with members of the security services. The idea was spreading in these circles that it was enough to organise unrest, such as unclaimed terrorist attacks in public places, in order to provoke fear within the population and thus push them to vote for political parties favourable to the order or even a strong state. The ghost of a right-wing coup was continually present in Italian politics and the two attempts, in 1967 and 1970, demonstrate that this was not just a fantasy of the Left.

The Crisis of the Left

After the end of the war, the PCI pursued a policy which reconciled both the need for the consolidation of Italian democracy and the persistence of a revolutionary feeling at the base of the party. The Liberation War that took place between September 1943 and 1945 in central and northern Italy did not turn, as in Yugoslavia, into a revolutionary war, and the myth of a 'betrayed resistance' was widespread in the activists' ranks, a feeling that would be passed down from generation to generation.

This revolutionary temptation resurfaced after the attack on Togliatti on 14 July 1948. Despite the call from the PCI leadership to remain calm, a pre-insurrectionary situation appeared in many regions. The workers' base began an impressive general strike with the occupation of the factories while former armed partisan formations reappeared in Biella, Valsesia and Casale Monferrato. communist militants attacked the Fiat factory, and some executives were taken hostage as weapons appeared. The armed clashes in Milan between communists and the police resulted in numerous injuries and the occupation of other factories. There were also clashes in Siena, Piombino, Taranto, Ferrara, Modena, Cagliari and La Spezia, while in Venice factories and bridges over the lagoon were occupied. In Genoa, the insurrectionary movement was even more extensive. Clashes between militants and police officers caused injuries, and even carabinieri and police officers were taken prisoner. The appearance of barricades forced the prefect to declare a state of siege. On the morning of 16 July, communist leaders took the decision to stop the revolutionary development and to stop the strike. Officially, the PCI had not given any insurrectionary directives, but rumours were circulating that officials like Pietro Secchia had been in favour of revolutionary action.[16]

For Togliatti, in view of the national and international context, the only possible policy for the PCI was to collaborate with the progressive sectors of the bourgeoisie to maintain the democratic institutions of Italy and to orient them towards changes of the economic and political structures. This evolution of the PCI, which became a defender of institutions, left a political space for those who reproached it for its commitment in the field of reforms but also for those who believed that revolutionary action could only ensure social transformation. The first signs of crises appeared in the 1960s with the transformations of the world communist movement following the 20th Congress of the Communist Party of the Soviet Union (CPSU) and the Sino-Soviet split, but above all because of the specific evolution of the PCI which increasingly made the choice of reformism which ensured electoral success and integrated it into the institutional system. This integration did not go without difficulty, as in 1956 when the PCI supported the invasion of Hungary by the Soviet armed forces, causing the departure of hundreds of intellectuals and the rupture with the PSI.

Resistance was also strong at the base of the PCI where for years the idea spread that Togliatti, who died in 1964, practised a double line, on the one hand respecting democratic rules, on the other waiting for the right moment to start the revolution. Rossana Rossanda rightly remarks:

> In fact, in our country, the social conflict has always been acute. He always carried elements of violence within him … I can testify to the high degree of violence of the political and social struggles between 1945 and 1959. They thus had their armed moments, because few were those who had obeyed the injunction of the American armed forces and the invitation of the National Liberation Committee to surrender, after July 1945, arms; many were those who kept them or concealed them.[17]

The radical wing of the PCI remained powerful and could be recognised in Giovanni Pesce and Pietro Secchia. Pesce first joined the International Brigades at the age of 18 to defend the Spanish Republic, and during the Second World War became one of the commanders of the *Gruppi d'Azione Patriottica* (Patriotic Action Groups or GAP), small clandestine formations that acted in the big cities of the north and perpetrated attacks against military targets and leaders of the fascist regime. In 1967, Pesce published *Senza tregua. La guerra dei GAP*, an urban guerrilla manual that quickly became a reference for those who would soon choose the path of armed struggle.[18] Secchia, for his part, was one of the founders of the PCI, and who, after spending many years in Mussolini's prisons, became during the war the political commissar of the Garibaldi Brigades, an army of 50,000 partisans, most of whom were communists. He was, nevertheless, gradually marginalised from 1956, when the reformist wing became the majority in the PCI. Two orientations coexisted within the PCI, and if it was true that the hard wing was in the minority, it was also true that the moneys from Moscow continued to arrive in Rome and that part of the PCI continued to have an attitude of 'proximity' with the Soviet bloc despite the different distances officially taken by the PCI from the CPSU.

The idea of Togliatti's double line, the weight of Secchia and Pesce, and the revolutionary dream of the old partisans imposed themselves in the early 1960s on new generations of militants. In April 1978 in *Il Manifesto*, Rossana Rossanda published the article 'The Family Album', in which she underlined the extent to which the relationship between the PCI and the armed struggle of the Left is evident. The exaltation of revolutionary violence for years by the communists fed the birth of the student and workers' revolts that the PCI hoped to be able to lead but also allowed the emergence of new revolutionary groups.[19]

The Italian Miracle

Despite the turmoil in political life, from the 1950s on, Italy experienced an economic miracle. The growth rate of the GDP was 5.5 percent per year between 1951 and 1958. Italian capitalism was in a phase of expansion and unprecedented growth which marked the passage from an essentially agricultural reality to an exporting industrial power in less than a decade.[20]

The economic gap between Italy and Northern Europe was narrowing, resulting in a rapprochement of lifestyles among Europeans. While Italy had only 342,000 cars at the start of the

1950s, there were around 15 million at the end of the 1970s. The construction of motorways and the development of the cars enabled Italians to travel, to discover their country and to indulge in tourism during their holidays. Homes were equipped with household appliances that improved the quality of life, while the diffusion of television – in 1965, one in two families had one – allowed the development of a homogeneous mass culture, symbolised by the success of the music festival of Sanremo. Above all, as in the rest of the Western world, a new social figure appeared in the Italy of the 1960s, the teenager, that period of life which separated childhood from entering the adult world and which tended to increase with longer schooling. Youth became a world in itself through its clothing tastes, the music it listened to, and its codes and rites that challenged the values and standards of adult society.[21]

This economic development, which allowed the emergence of a consumer society, was only possible because companies demanded strong increases in productivity rates from workers, while inflation, used by governments to support competitiveness, favoured investments but also the stagnation of real wage levels. Industry then adopted the Fordist mode of production and the massive introduction of labour-intensive assembly lines. This resulted in emigration from the south to the large industrial cities of the north, the depopulation of the countryside to the cities. From 1951 to 1971, more than 9 million Italians experienced the rural exodus and the departure for the cities of the north.[22]

These economic and social upheavals undermined the country's traditional structures and created new inequalities. The arrival of migrants from the south pushed up rental prices in northern cities due to the high demand for housing. Workers were forced to spend the night in railway stations while thousands slept crammed into cramped rooms. The workers coming from the Mezzogiorno, accustomed to a peasant and communal reality, had to face the hectic rhythms of the factories, get used to the dominant values of industrial cities, to the logic of profit and individualism. These transformations could appear to many Italians as a collective and individual trauma. This was especially true for the industrial proletariat which was profoundly changed by economic transformations. It was becoming both younger and less tied to the traditions of the workers' movement. In this context, the traditional unions were no longer able to respond to the demands of these new workers. As Simona Colarizi notes, 'the economic and cultural growth of the Italian population after WWII is too fast and difficult to manage'.[23] This observation is particularly true for Italian universities.

The Students of 1968

It was in American universities, in particular that of Berkeley in California, that a youth revolt began in 1964, which rapidly spread throughout the world. Young people contested the values of an individualist and conformist society, criticised the authoritarianism of the older generations and traditional institutions. The political dimension of this revolt was manifested in the commitment against the war and American imperialism in Vietnam[24] but also in the denunciation of Soviet totalitarianism which was expressed with the crushing of the Prague Spring by the Warsaw Pact troops. The May 68 in France, with its dream of a union between the workers' movement and the thousands of students marching in the streets of Paris, embodied this need for change which was imposed in all the industrialised countries of the West. To overthrow the capitalist consumer

Fighting between Neo-Nazis and far-left students in Rome of 1968. (Albert Grandolini collection)

A scene from what became known as the Battle of Valle Giulia, moments before students assaulted officers of the Police Celere. (Albert Grandolini collection)

society, young people were rediscovering Marxism, but a Marxism different from that of the traditional communist parties. It was a Marxism revisited by the writings of Marcuse, the criticisms of the Situationists, the *Little Red Book* of Mao Zedong, the revolutionary romanticism of the Vietnamese resistance, and of the Palestinian and Latin American guerrillas whose heroic figure was embodied in Che Guevara and its famous slogan 'Create two, three, many Vietnams'.

Italy was no exception to this youthful desire for change, of which universities were the melting pot. As in France or in West Germany, the Italian university system had changed little as it had to cope during the 1960s with a very strong increase in enrolments. The number of students thus increased from 139,000 in 1955 to 405,000 in 1965 and 935,000 in 1975.[25] And these new generations were challenging an education that had changed little and regulations that left them little position in the management of university life.

The radicalisation of the youth appeared in April 1966 when the death of a socialist student at the University of Rome, killed by a group of neo-fascists, sparked protests across the country with clashes between the students and the police in Trento.[26] The movement gained momentum in 1967 and 1968 when the government planned to reform the university system and increase tuition fees at the Catholic University of Milan and the Trento University Institute of Social Sciences. Above all, students were calling for a reform of teaching methods which they considered too rigid. In Trento, at the start of the 1967–1968 academic year, sociology students, including Renato Curcio and Margherita Cagol, wrote a 'Manifesto for a Negative University', which presented the university as an instrument in the hands of the ruling class in order to perpetuate its power. The birth of a new university was therefore theorised, capable of opposing capitalism but also of finding a socialist path with concrete proposals. The Trento University was then transformed into a 'Negative University', where, with enthusiasm and self-management, the students established new teaching methods. They gave up specifically university demands and moved towards political work by seeking to link up with workers' struggles.[27] After Trento, Pisa University was occupied in February 1967, that of Milan in November and that of Turin in January 1968.[28]

The student revolt took a new turn with the Battle of Valle Giulia in Rome on 1 March 1968. About 3,000 young people attempted to seize a university building in the Valle Giulia gardens. The police intervened, but unlike what usually happened, the students did not back down from, but instead faced a direct physical confrontation and counterattack. Police vehicles were burnt, policemen beaten and deprived of their weapons. The toll of the clash was over 200 wounded, most of whom were police. In the eyes of other students in the country, the young people of Valle Giulia had become a role model. For many, it was also the demonstration of the real revolutionary possibilities of the student movement.[29] From this point on, the rallies and the attitude of the demonstrators changed as armed and well-trained security services emerged. The violence of the street clashes was on the rise. In Milan, on 8 June, violent confrontations took place between the carabinieri and the students who wanted to seize the headquarters of the conservative newspaper, *Corriere della Sera*.[30] On 31 December, in Marina di Pietrasanta, near Pisa, the police severely repressed a student demonstration. They did not hesitate to shoot, and injured 14 people including a 17-year-old who remained paralysed for life[31]. This repression, the state's only response to the student protest, accentuated the choice of a section of the youth to turn to violence.

The Workers' Revolt of 1969

If 1968 was the year of students, 1969 was the year of workers. In Milan, Turin and Genoa, the centre of gravity of social struggles was moving from the universities to the doors of the big Fiat, Alfa Romeo, Magneti Marelli and SIT-Siemens factories. It was between September and December 1969 that the workers' social explosion began in these large industrial centres in the north of the country. This *Autunno caldo* (Hot Autumn) began with the renewal of 32 collective labour agreements affecting 5 million workers in industry, agriculture and other sectors. On this occasion, the workers were determined to make their demands heard, as wages were among the lowest in Europe and working conditions generally poor.

In July, in Turin and its province, strikes broke out while clashes took place with the police. On the 3rd, Fiat workers, joined by students, fought the police in Corso Traiano. Turin, on this day, was the place of violent urban guerrilla events. On 2 September, when Fiat finally decided to suspend 25,000 workers, the conflict spread to the entire Turin–Milan–Genoa industrial triangle. Strikes spread to other factories and workers' demonstrations began to leave factories for city centres.[32]

On 10 October, large demonstrations of metallurgists took place across the country. Strikes also affected other categories of workers such as construction, postal and telegraph, and railway workers, while in the big cities a movement to occupy vacant houses was growing. On 19 November, during a demonstration in Milan, clashes

A meeting of workers at the Fiat factory in 1969. (Author's collection)

Officers of the Police Celere facing Fiat workers at the Corso Traiano, in Turin, on 3 July 1969. (Author's collection)

Another wave of demonstrations that culminated in riots and severe clashes with the security forces occurred in Milano, in late November 1969. (Albert Grandolini collection)

Police officers and carabinieri – both armed with submachine guns – in front of a factory in northern Italy in 1973. (Albert Grandolini collection)

were violent and a policeman was killed.[33] Strikes and factory occupations continued until the Piazza Fontana bombing on 12 December 1969.

But the magnitude of the Hot Autumn went beyond the traditional industrial conflicts that accompanied important social negotiations. It was a great collective movement whose forms, demands and actions broke with those of the unions. It relied on what was then called the 'mass worker', that is to say, unskilled assembly line workers who had left the rural south to work in the industrial north. Virtually devoid of trade union traditions, often despised, they organised themselves into *Comitati Unitari di Base* (CUB or Basic Units Committees). The aim of these organisations was not to replace the unions, but to force it to follow the advice of the assemblies, often improvised, where the workers met and could speak freely. Often, numerous students participated in these assemblies in front of the factories' doors. When the CUB appeared, Study Groups were also formed, notably at Pirelli, SIT-Siemens and IBM factories, which brought together white-collar workers. It was the first time that they had taken part alongside the workers in a confrontation with the employers on positions far removed from those of the unions.[34] The protest thus spilled over into the workers' and student sectors.

The main demands of the CUB related to the elimination of dangerous jobs, the reduction of working hours, the end of piecework and the demand for new hires. But alongside these demands, among the most radical elements of the CUB, the idea of a 'proletarian justice' which had to punish the employers' executives who were too zealous and hostile to the workers, was also beginning to appear. The forms of workers' struggles were also becoming more radical, employing the slowdown, demonstrations inside the factory and direct negotiations without the participation of unions. Violence was also present with the use of sabotage, the beating of executives and the destruction of their cars.[35]

While workers' unrest shook the day-to-day life in the factories, the official unions travelled to Rome to negotiate and sign industrial agreements with the state and the Confindustria, the employers' union. Wages were increased and working time reduced to 40 hours per week. The Hot Autumn finally led to the vote of the 'Workers' Statute', one of the most favourable to employees in a Western European country.[36]

The unprecedented success of the Hot Autumn battles reflected a balance of power in favour of the working class that was felt throughout the 1970s. Thus, at Fiat in Turin, social conflicts continued intermittently until 1980. If for the far-left organisations, the signing of the agreements represented a defeat, since the workers' agitation which was expressed was hijacked by the hated unions considered to be the secular arm of capital, the meeting between the student protests and workers' mobilisation suggested the possibility of a revolutionary process which, in the short term, was capable of overthrowing the social and cultural order. This feeling was reinforced by the rise of political violence. From 1969 to 1971, the number of crimes committed during demonstrations or for political reasons amounted to more than 83,000, and violations of the law on weapons to 771.[37]

With the Hot Autumn of 1969, fears of a changing society, already troubled by the student protests of 1967–1968, were heightened. Social conflict arose in a situation of blockage and fragility of the political system. The DC could not turn to the Right, after the failed experience of the Tambroni government in 1960, nor to the Left, especially since the increase in the electoral weight of the PCI during the elections of 19 May 1968. This situation provoked a reaction of fear and concern in the more moderate part of the population, which viewed with concern the difficulties of the country.

2
THE BIRTH OF THE BRIGATE ROSSE

The first episode of armed struggle on the Left took place on 5 October 1970 with the kidnapping of the entrepreneur Sergio Gadolla in Genoa by the *XXII Ottobre* group. This underground organisation was born in 1969 in a context marked by wildcat strikes and strong social tensions in which many far-left groups emerged.[1] Among them was the group that gave birth to the BR, a formation originally peaceful which gradually slipped into armed struggle as the Piazza Fontana bombing on 12 December 1969 opened a new phase in Italian history.

The Extra-parliamentary Left

The first far-left movements appeared in the early 1960s, after the fall of the Tambroni government, when concrete prospects for reform and democratic enlargement of the power system opened up. They were born on the initiative of groups of communist dissidents, left-wing socialist intellectuals and radical Marxists who debated revolutionary perspectives in Italy. The deepest and most effective impetus for the development of this 'revolutionary Left' came from the internal contradiction in the PCI between the revolutionary ideology of Marxism-Leninism which permeated the culture and mentality of the militants and ensured its hegemony over the intellectual world, and the reformist politics that it led on a daily basis. To get out of this dilemma, some were looking for a path in political and doctrinal extremism. They wished to leave the reformist practice of the PCI by a return to the original purity and to the revolutionary theory of Marx and Lenin.

Thus, in October 1961 appeared the first issue of *Quaderni Rossi* and in 1962 the first Marxist-Leninist group and the magazine *Quaderni Piacentini*.[2] Within the PCI, Luigi Pintor and Rossana Rossanda founded, in June 1969, *Il Manifesto*, a journal of political research but above all of protest to the Left of the official line, the editors of which would be excluded from the PCI two years later. In this far-left, the idea was developing, through the example of the Algerian and Cuban revolutions and Vietnamese guerrilla warfare, that the overwhelming superiority of the superpowers, in terms of technology and military capabilities, was not sufficient to stem the revolutionary movements. The latter had to coordinate to give

A demonstration organised by the *Lotta Continua*. (Albert Grandolini collection)

A demonstration organised by the *Potere Operaio*. (Albert Grandolini collection)

Mara Cagol and Renato Curcio, in the late 1960s. (Albert Grandolini collection)

birth to a new proletarian internationalism, capable of undermining the peaceful coexistence between the United States and the Soviet Union, and at the same time promoting an insurrectionary strategy on a world scale. Thus, in the second half of the 1960s, the explosion of student protest in Europe and North America was accompanied by the conviction that the revolution was achievable even in the heart of the West.

Nevertheless, the different far-left groups, which were of different ideological inspiration – some were Maoists, Trotskyists or Guevarists – had different analyses of the use of violence, even if all justified its necessity and its use to overthrow the existing order. For *Avanguardia Operaia* (Worker Vanguard or AO), which was born from the unification of various Milanese groups in 1968, the most important thing was to create a 'Revolutionary Marxist-Leninist Party', a process which could only be gradual and long, which kept it apart from the temptation of armed struggle.[3]

The most important organisation of the extra-parliamentary Left, *Lotta Continua* (Continuous Struggle or LC), was founded in 1969 from the ashes of the newspaper *Il Potere Operaio* from Pisa, on the initiative of its leader Adriano Sofri. The LC, with its libertarian spirit, appeared to be the closest to the spontaneous spirit of 1968, the most allergic to the idea of bureaucracy. Unlike AO, who had never theorised or practised violence except for street clashes, for LC, mass violence was the natural response to what it saw as the ontological violence of the bourgeois system.[4] It therefore participated in countless street fights with the police and neo-fascists, and its security service was one of the most violent and ruthless. Without ever having chosen the transition to armed struggle, LC brought a contribution to its genesis by its exaltation of the practice of street fights and the theorisation of revolutionary armed struggle.[5] This contradiction between discourse and practice also led LC activists to leave the group to form the *Nuclei Armati Proletari* (Armed Proletarian Cells or NAP). Others would choose the armed struggle later, after the dissolution of LC in 1976, by joining *Prima Linea* (Front Line or PL) and to a small extent the BR.[6]

Another important group within the extra-parliamentary Left was *Potere Operaio* (Workers Power or Pot Op), a national organisation with a presence in major urban centres, particularly in the north-central area, which had thousands of activists. In addition to its numerical weight, the strength of this group lay in a leadership composed of intellectuals, Franco Piperno, Oreste Scalzone and Toni Negri, capable of carrying out intense theoretical activity. In the struggles of the autumn of 1969, Pot Op tried to radicalise the movement by exaggerating the demands, proposing the revolutionary concept of salary unrelated to productivity, and the refusal that work is a human need. Subsequently, it advocated 'hard struggles' in factories with strikes and sabotage, and in neighbourhoods with the occupation of houses, and the refusal to pay bills and tram or metro tickets.[7] If the group thus extolled 'mass illegality' as an instrument which served to entrench the consciousness and the practice of armed struggle, the absence of an insurrection encouraged it to doubt its initial assumptions, especially since the armed struggle remained a very limited phenomenon in the organisation which did not build clandestine military structures, only a security service.[8] The bad prospects and especially the internal divisions of Pot Op led to its dissolution in June 1973. Members of the group, such as Mario Morucci and Adriana Faranda, then joined the BR.[9]

The Collettivo Politico Metropolitano and the Appartamento

At the end of 1968, Curcio and Cagol, who were particularly active at the University of Trento, left the city for Verano where they joined an anti-imperialist movement called the Information Centre which published the *Lavoro Politico* newspaper.[10] This newspaper was very critical of the partisans of violence, in particular those who advocated urban guerrilla warfare, because it believed that the moment was not yet clearly revolutionary. To achieve the seizure of power, according to the newspaper, a true Marxist-Leninist party had to be founded. A few months later, the young couple moved to Milan.[11] It was in this city that the *Collettivo Politico Metropolitano* (Metropolitan

Mario Moretti. (Albert Grandolini collection)

Alberto Franceschini (left) and Renato Curcio in a courthouse. (Author's collection)

Political Collective or CPM) was formed on 8 September 1969. Among the founders were, in addition to Curcio and Cagol, Raffale De Mori, Mario Moretti, Corrado Simioni, Franco Troiano, Vanni Mulinaris and Italo Saugo. The goal of the CPM was to coordinate student worker committees, Study Groups and CUBs in order to bring conflicts out of factories and spread them throughout the city. The struggle against capitalism was therefore seen as a long-term process in which it was necessary to denounce the violence of the state, intrinsic to the capitalist system. The CPM therefore did not yet consider itself as an organisation which had to lead the revolutionary process, but as a stage in its constitution.[12]

It was at the end of 1969 that the CPM came into contact with a group of young people from Reggio-Emilia, many of whom had been activists within the Italian Communist Youth Federation or the PCI before leaving them or being excluded because of their hostility to the party's moderate policies. These young activists breaking away from the PCI, including Prospero Gallinari and Alberto Franceschini, formed a Worker-Student Political Collective which took the name of the *Appartamento* (Apartment/Flat) Group in reference to the room where they met.[13] Between 1969 and 1970, hundreds of young people from socialism, communism and anarchism passed through the *Appartamento*, but also young Catholics such as Roberto Ognibene. Close to the PCI hard wing, some of these members received military training from former partisans who were also opposed to the giving up of the revolutionary line by the new communist leadership.[14]

Soon, the contacts between the *Appartamento* and the CPM members became closer. The former began to travel frequently to Milan, while members of the CPM went to Reggio-Emilia. The CPM thus gradually extended its influence and became, in particular in Milan, an organisation present in dozens of factories, schools and well set up in working-class neighbourhoods.[15]

Piazza Fontana and the Emergence of Armed Struggle

It was in the atmosphere of workers' and student struggles at the end of 1969, that on 12 December at 4:37 p.m., in the central hall of the Banca Nazionale dell'Agricoltura in Piazza Fontana in Milan, a bomb exploded killing 16 people and injuring 87. The dead were all bank customers, ordinary citizens. At the same time, other bombs exploded in Rome at the Banca Nazionale del Lavoro, at the Altar of the Fatherland and near the Risorgimento museum leaving 13 injured while another bomb, in the Banca Commerciale Italiana in Milan, was found unexploded.[16] Today, if the responsibility of the neo-fascists in this attack is no longer in doubt, the debate is still open as to whether they were manipulated by the secret services, or even whether the CIA and the Americans did not play the role of puppeteers.

This tragedy opened a new period in the history of Italy, that of terror because, for the first time, an attack killed people. This was indeed not the first. On 25 January 1969, for example, a bomb exploded at the Palace of Justice in Padua, while on 15 April, still in the same city, a bomb destroyed the office of the rector of the university. In April, and especially in August 1969, there were bombs placed in first-class compartments of railway trains all over Italy causing a dozen casualties.[17]

The scale of the Piazza Fontana bombing led to an end to the workers' unrest of the Hot Autumn and intensified the repression against leftist forces. For this, the authorities used articles inherited from the fascist penal code, such as those which punished subversive propaganda and incitement to social hatred, to seek the culprits of the Milan attack within the ranks of the Left, in particular among

Police officers inspecting the damage after the Piazza Fontana bombing. (Albert Grandolini collection)

The scene inside the bank at the Piazza Fontana after its bombing. (Albert Grandolini collection)

Giangiacomo Feltrinelli, one of the masterminds of the idea that led to the establishment of the *Brigate Rosse*. (Albert Grandolini collection)

the anarchists. It was in this context that another tragedy soon occurred with the death of anarchist Giuseppe Pinelli, who fell from a window of the Milan police station on 15 December during an interrogation. A few hours after the incident, the authorities said that Pinelli committed suicide and that his action amounted to an admission of guilt for the Piazza Fontana bombing. This version was quickly revealed to be false and Police Commissioner Giuseppe Calabresi, who was interrogating Pinelli, was suspected of having defenestrated him.

The repression against the Left was taken very seriously. The PCI activated all available channels to prepare for the possible exfiltration of its leadership abroad while the far-left movements, LC and Pot Op, formed their security services made up of armed militants.[18] For the Left, the Piazza Fontana bombing confirmed fears of a future 'fascist coup' as happened in neighbouring Greece in 1967. The dominant idea of a violence necessary as a means of political struggle was growing. Then was added the denunciation of a state that opposed the revolutionary process by using neo-fascist violence. This was notably the case of Giangiacomo Feltrinelli for whom anti-fascist self-defence became a necessity to respond to the danger of a fascist drift of the state.

At the end of the 1960s, Feltrinelli was a major figure on the far-left. Coming from a wealthy family, partisan during the war, then a member of the PCI, he founded a publishing house in 1954 which rose to fame in 1958 with the publication of Boris Pasternak's unpublished novel, *Doctor Zhivago*. But Feltrinelli also distinguished himself by publishing and distributing revolutionary literature. At the same time, he met Fidel Castro in 1964 and then Régis Debray in Bolivia after the death of Che Guevara in 1967. He also made many trips to Eastern Europe and in 1968 he had the project of making Sardinia a Mediterranean Cuba. He quickly gave up his plan, the island having many NATO bases on its territory.[19]

In the aftermath of the Piazza Fontana bombing, Feltrinelli went into hiding. He considered the attack to be the work of the far-right and expected, at the instigation of the United States, an imminent coup led by neo-fascists and the armed forces. He felt the only way was to resume the Maquis and the urban guerrilla warfare as during the Second World War. Under the pseudonym Osvaldo Ivaldi, Feltrinelli founded the *Gruppi d'Azione Partigiana* (Partisan Action Groups or GAP) and wanted to form guerrilla bases in Sardinia, and in the Apennines, from Emilia to Liguria. In the meantime, his GAP, organised by Giuseppe Saba, set fire to the PSI headquarters in Genoa on 24 April 1970, then the headquarters of the United States consulate on 3 May.[20]

Feltrinelli placed his organisation in a global framework that went beyond the Italian context to fit into the genealogy of international communism.[21] This vision, which placed the armed struggle in Italy in the historical and geographical continuity of a larger struggle, was far from gaining unanimity within the far-left born in the 1960s, which was very critical of the socialist camp as they were also the BR's founders. It was this conviction of the need for Soviet support for the victory of the revolution in the West that explained Feltrinelli's many trips to Czechoslovakia and East Germany as well as his contacts with the Soviet embassy in Rome.[22]

The Foundation of BR

For the CPM, the Piazza Fontana tragedy was also a rupture. The collective, whose activities until then were confined to theoretical debates and cultural actions such as the organisation of plays or artistic exhibitions, was shaken by the attack, as recalled by Curcio, who was also arrested for a few hours by the police after the bombing.[23] For Mario Moretti, the 12 December drama was an attack against the workers' and revolutionary movement which now had to defend itself.[24]

FOGLIO DI LOTTA

sinistra PROLETARIA

ANNO III N°15 GENNAIO 1971

ORGANIZZIAMO LA NUOVA RESISTENZA!

Mantenere l'offensiva. Rimanere all'attacco. Unificare le lotte.

A page from the *Sinistra Proletaria* newspaper of 1971. (Author's collection)

Nevertheless, the question of the armed struggle within the CPM arose a few weeks before the Piazza Fontana bombing. From 1 to 4 November 1969, the CPM, which brought together about 70 people, met in Chiavari in a Catholic boarding house called Stella Maris. It decided to transform into a more organised structure which took the name of *Sinistra Proletaria* (Proletarian Left) and to write a newspaper of the same name.[25] The final document of the meeting, called the 'yellow book' and entitled *Lotta rivoluzionaria nella metropoli*, for the first time considered recourse to armed struggle.[26]

But the testimonies of the BR leaders were divergent concerning the place held by the question of the armed struggle in the debates in Chiavari. While Curcio gave a long speech on the need to enter a new political phase by adopting a better organisational structure, Franceschini argued that it was not about armed struggle but only about a possible going underground. He thus suggested that this choice showed a defensive rather than an offensive attitude, arguing that the decision to engage in armed struggle was taken in response to the Piazza Fontana bombing. Moretti contradicts this interpretation because he considers that this going underground was an offensive act: 'We do not go underground because we are wanted by the police … It is not a decision in defence, but in attack. We are not running away: on the contrary. By hiding, we will build an armed proletarian power.'[27] This statement is reinforced by the testimony of Gallinari who explains that the CPM was preparing for the use of violence from autumn 1969. He thus tells that an activist from Milan came to Reggio-Emilia to teach the *Appartamento* Group how to make and use Molotov cocktails.[28]

While it is difficult to say that the Chiavari meeting was the moment of choice for armed struggle, it is certainly important for thinking about the CPM's future. Likewise, the Piazza Fontana bombing constituted for its members a confirmation of the correctness of their ideas and their projects. Chiavari was also often presented as the birth certificate of the BR, but the reality was more complex. At the beginning of 1970, hard workers' struggles still took place in the north of the country against the loss of many jobs. CPM activists tried to insert themselves into these struggles, in particular by distributing a leaflet at the SIT-Siemens factory in Milan in July. At the same time, the newspaper *Sinistra Proletaria* announced the birth of autonomous workers' organisations called the Red Brigades which had to both carry out propaganda and fight the enemies of the working class.

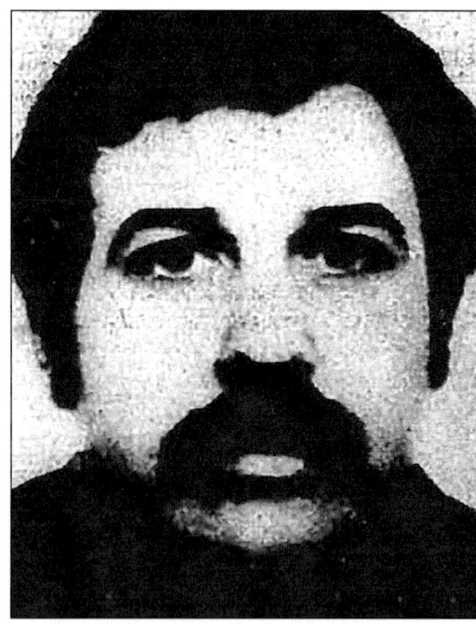

Renato Curcio, in a photograph from the early 1970s. (Albert Grandolini collection)

On 17 August 1970, 78 delegates of *Sinistra Proletaria* coming from Turin, Milan, Trento, Reggio-Emilia and Rome met in Costaferrata, near Pecorile in the Apennines.[29] The question of the transition to armed struggle was no longer debated, but it was the modalities of its implementation that were discussed. Curcio proposed a gradual transition from factories, through small cells but still linked to the mass and to 'basic realities'. The concrete aim was to create in the Milan factories semi-clandestine formations called Red Brigades to prepare armed propaganda actions and support a long-lasting political and civil war.[30] Curcio would later relate that the objectives of this armed struggle were modest, such as burning the cars of industrial executives and that it did not contemplate the use of firearms. Nevertheless, his proposal provoked a debate. For Simioni, in fact, it was necessary to create, alongside the Red Brigades, a completely clandestine organisation intended exclusively for military activities and ready for armed confrontation regardless of social conflicts. This disagreement caused the departure of a group of around 20 activists, including Corrado Alunni and Mario Moretti.[31]

These departures did not allow the conflicts to be resolved within the Coordination Committee of *Sinistra Proletaria*, formed after the meeting at Pecorile and composed of Curcio, Simioni, Cagol, Raffaele De Mori, Duccio Berio, Franco Troiano, Gaio Di Silvestro, Alberto Pinotti and Franceschini. Simioni began to lead the activity of a secret group and organised, without telling Curcio and Franceschini, an attack in Athens against the United States Embassy, in which Maria Elena Angeloni and Giorgio Christou Tsdiroukis were killed in the explosion of the bomb they were to plant. Simioni had asked Margherita Cagol to participate in the attack, but she refused. This episode caused the break-up. Simioni, Troiano, Berio and others left *Sinistra Proletaria* to organise the Superclan, which Gallinari and Vanni Mulinaris also joined.[32]

If these departures signified the end of *Sinistra Proletaria*, replaced by the BR, they were reinforced with the arrival of militants from the Luglio 60 group, from the Lorenteggio district and other groups from the Giambellino and Quarto Oggiaro districts of Milan. In the spring 1971, it was the turn of the Alunni and Moretti group, who continued their political action at SIT-Siemens to join the BR again.[33]

Feltrinelli's Failure

At the time of the BR's birth, Feltrinelli was in contact with various groups then close to the armed struggle such as LC and Pot Op. He sought to 'create a People's Liberation Army' and, in January 1971, he met again the leaders of these two organisations to discuss the possibility of their unification.[34] These discussions failed. LC did not want to engage in armed struggle while Pot Op favoured the creation of a political organisation and a military nucleus separate from each other.

Feltrinelli met more success with the first organisation of armed struggle to have emerged, in Italy, the *XXII Ottobre* group, founded in Genoa in 1969 by Mario Rossi, Augusto Viel, Rinaldo Fiorani and Silvio Malagoli. This group organised the burning of the properties of certain Genoese businessmen, but for the organisation of the kidnapping of Sergio Gadolla from 5 to 10 October 1970, it called on dubious characters such as the former MSI activist Diego Vandelli, Gianfranco Astara and Adolfo Sanguineti, who later denounced their comrades.[35] Feltrinelli managed to integrate this group into his organisation which became the third column of GAP, the other two being in Milan and Trento.[36]

Feltrinelli also met representatives of BR such as Curcio, whom he had known since 1968 and to whom he provided brochures of the Uruguayan revolutionaries Tupamaros, and Carlos Marighella's *Minimanual of the Urban Guerrilla*.[37] Curcio and Franceschini discussed their differences with him. The latter was in fact a partisan of a Guevarist-type guerrilla warfare based on small avant-garde detachments – a conception of armed struggle opposed to that of the BR who wanted to lead the fight in the metropolises.[38] Feltrinelli thought of the armed struggle in terms of relation to the state and of international revolution, while the BR wanted to inscribe their actions in daily social struggles. Above all, unlike the GAPs, the BR only gave secondary importance to the anti-fascist struggle when it was not associated with social themes.[39]

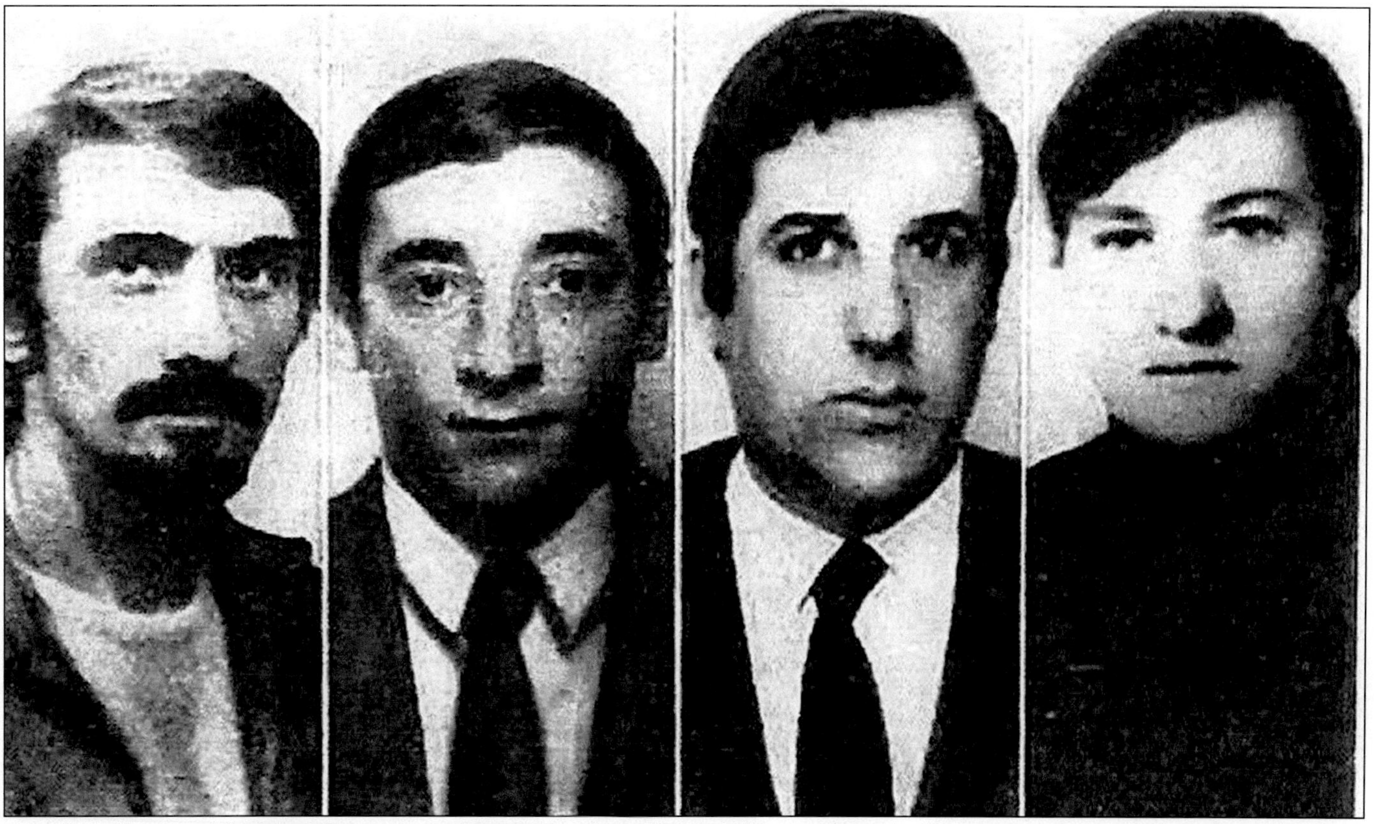

Four alleged leaders of the *Brigate Rosse*, seen in photographs released by the Italian security authorities in May 1974, from left to right: Piero Morlacchi, Mario Moretti, Renato Curcio, and Alfredo Bonavita. (Albert Grandolini collection)

Despite the disagreements and the desire of the BR to maintain their autonomy, in particular by refusing the money that Feltrinelli offered them, there was nevertheless a collaboration with the GAP as shown by a common claim after the destruction of the car of a neo-fascist in Quarto Oggiaro on 14 July 1971.[40] Feltrinelli also played an instructor role with the BR in weapons handling and liaison with foreign armed groups.[41]

The birth of the BR went fairly unnoticed in the midst of the proliferation of far-left groups that existed at the time. The organisation was modestly staffed, it was based only in Milan, did not have any talented intellectuals as LC did, nor a known leader such as Feltrinelli with the GAP. It was in this relative anonymity that the BR took their first steps and committed their first actions.

3
THE PATH OF URBAN GUERRILLA WARFARE, 1970–1974

The beginnings of the BR were modest. The organisation was defining a strategy to support workers' unrest and orient it towards forms of organised violent action. They therefore deployed their efforts where this agitation existed; the factories and working-class neighbourhoods. Armed actions were then limited, but this phase did not prevent a gradual escalation of violence which amplified the audience of the BR and also pushed the state to react.

Armed Propaganda

At the end of the summer of 1971, in a brochure, the BR explained the strategic choice of armed struggle as the only possible response to the offensive led by the bourgeoisie against the proletariat. For the BR, the bourgeoisie, faced with the social and political crisis, had only one answer, the militarisation of the system with the establishment of an authoritarian 'neo-Gaullist' regime, which was developing under an apparent democracy. For the BR, the armed struggle had already started and it was the bourgeoisie that initiated it, as shown by the Piazza Fontana bombing. The problem for the proletariat was then to create an instrument capable of responding to this attack. The BR saw themselves as that tool which, within social struggles, sought to unite and mobilise the masses around a vanguard which had to carry out a series of violent actions, aimed at instilling a revolutionary consciousness in the working class. It was a question of radicalising the workers' struggles, of creating an alternative power in the factories and working-class neighbourhoods, of forming an elite from which would be born a real fighting communist party.[1] In the long-term, once the goal of building a proletarian counter-power, an armed party, had been achieved, the real revolution against the regime could begin.[2]

For the BR, the armed vanguard was not the armed wing of a disarmed mass movement, but rather its culmination, its place of unification. For this they wanted to be an organisation made up of

A mobile police unit in the process of dispersing another demonstration. (Albert Grandolini collection)

both politicians and guerrillas. This was a break with the vision of the revolution in two stages as defined by the Leninist tradition of the Comintern: first, the patient accumulation of forces through propaganda, then, when the conditions were right, the armed insurrection. For the BR, these two phases of preparation and armed struggle should form only one. They therefore rejected the idea of a division between political and military work where the second was subject to the first and wanted to unite politics and armed practice in a single tactic, armed propaganda.[3]

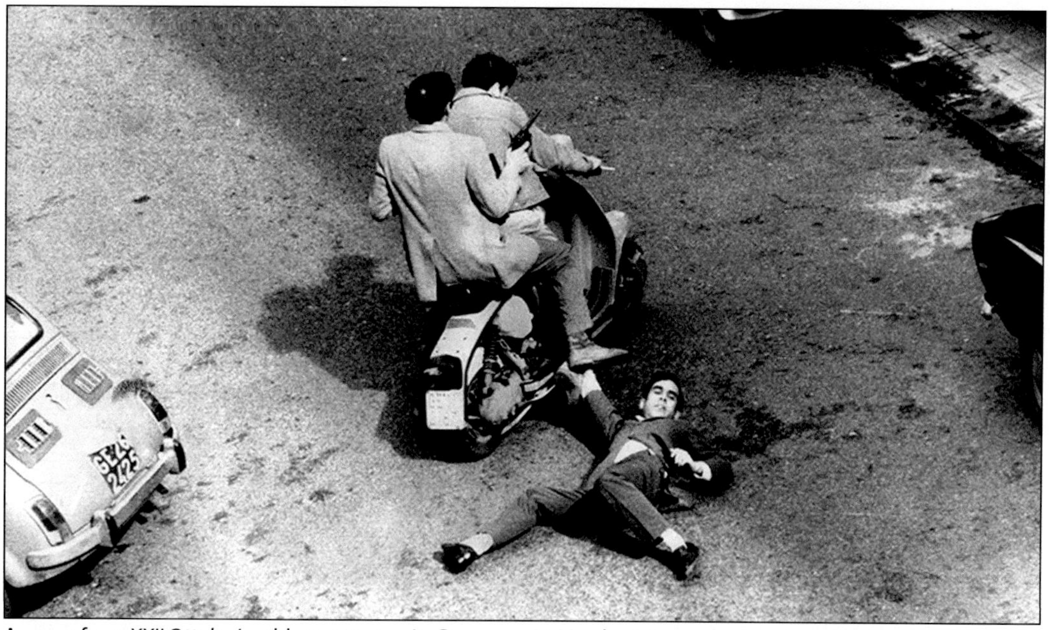

A scene from *XXII Ottobre*'s robbery attempt in Genoa on 26 March 1971. (Author's collection)

The strategy of armed propaganda deployed by the BR therefore sought, through exemplary violent actions at the level of the factories, to 'root in the struggling proletarian masses the principle: you will not have political power if you do not have military power, educate through partisan struggle the proletarian and revolutionary Left to resistance, to armed struggle'.[4] It had to therefore allow the first forms of armed organisation to take root in the daily struggle of factories and neighbourhoods, and to maintain the popular mobilisation at a high level. It thus represented the premise of the strategic confrontation, the struggle for power.

The Armed Struggle in the Factories

In the spring of 1970, in the Lorenteggio district of Milan, leaflets signed by the BR appeared, accompanied by the design of a five-pointed star. The text announced that 'The red autumn has already started, the deadline for a decisive struggle in the struggle for power … Against the institutions … the most determined and conscious part of the proletariat in the struggle has already started to fight to build a new legality, a new power'.[5] On 14 August, leaflets appeared at the SIT-Siemens factory which contained insults aimed against 'bastards' and 'executioners'. A few days later, the BR showed up again when a motorcyclist passing in front of the SIT-Siemens factory, threw around a hundred leaflets containing the names, surnames and addresses of the company's executives and workers accused of having connections with the boss. This time, the call to action was precise, the people mentioned in the leaflet 'must be struck by proletarian revenge'.[6]

The choice of SIT-Siemens was explained by the presence in this company of a large part of the BR's founders such as Moretti, Alunni, Franceschini, Fabrizio Pelli, Ognibene and Piero Bertolazzi.[7] In addition to SIT-Siemens, the BR were establishing themselves at the Pirelli factory, in the industrial area of Sesto San Giovanni, but also at the Marelli, Falck and Breda factories, which soon each had a Red Brigade. The first 10 brigades of the organisation were formed from members of CUBs and Study Groups at Pirelli and SIT-Siemens. Many people joined these brigades, which were then open, and not clandestine groups where it was possible to campaign for a certain time before leaving them. The BR were also moving to Alfa Romeo factories and to the popular districts of Giambellino and Quarto Oggiaro. They then benefited from the sympathy of many workers and maintained relations with CUBs, social centres and worker-student committees.[8]

The BR's first violent action took place on 17 September 1970, at Via Moretto da Brescia in Milan, when a rudimentary bomb set fire to the garage where Giuseppe Leoni, Director of Personnel of SIT-Siemens, parked his car.[9] The action was claimed with two pieces of paper left behind, bearing the words 'Brigate Rosse' and a few days later by leaflets deposited in the locker rooms of the factory. At the Pirelli factory, leaflets also appeared with a 'proscription list'.[10] At the end of November, a car belonging to the head of the factory's surveillance service was set on fire in retaliation for the dismissal of a *Confederazione Generale Italiana del Lavoro* (Italian General Confederation of Labour or CGIL) worker, a former partisan commander.[11]

The BR's armed propaganda tactics, which mixed threats and attacks against property, continued in the following months. The Italian press began to speak about them after eight incendiary bombs were placed under trucks on the test track of the Pirelli factory of Lainate in Milan on the night of 25 January 1971. Three of the eight bombs exploded causing significant serious damage.[12] Along with industrial targets, the BR attacked those they called 'fascists', a category that included both MSI and DC militants. This allowed them to get out of the factory sector and broaden the front line of confrontation while also raising its level. On 23 April 1971, cars belonging to two far-right activists were set on fire.[13] The BR also engaged in a different type of action – armed robbery – in order to finance these activities. Thus, with the collaboration of the GAP of Trento, a hold-up in Pergine near Lake Garda was carried out by Moretti, Morlacchi and Marco Pisetta.[14]

The authorities then began to take an interest in the BR. In December 1970, the Prefect of Milan, Libero Mazza, informed the Minister of the Interior of the existence of the BR and gave the names of their most famous activists, Curcio, Simioni and Troaiano. The Milan police quickly identified one of the perpetrators of the Lainate attack, the painter Enrico Castellani, who was found in possession of BR documentation and a timer system. Castellani, however, was not arrested and fled. In the eyes of the authorities, the actions of the BR appeared indeed modest in the face of the violence of other groups.[15] On 26 March, during a robbery, an employee of the Istituto

Autonomo Case Popolari in Genoa was killed by the *XXII Ottobre* group whose leader, Mario Rossi, was captured.[16]

The authorities' lack of interest in the BR allowed them to develop. Activists easily entered factories, especially Fiat factories, which were becoming one of the main locations for the BR who were trying to organise sympathisers and take action there. This situation nevertheless provoked a reaction from the Fiat management which resulted in dismissals or to the transfer of the most politicised workers to 'isolated' establishments.[17]

The First Crisis

In the first months of 1972, the BR continued their actions. Between 20 January and 19 February, they set fire to cars belonging to MSI leaders in Milan as well as the Lux cinema where a meeting of the neo-fascist party was to take place. On 18 February, they struck in Turin by throwing an incendiary device at the headquarters of a moderate trade union and, on 27 February, they entered the home of the deputy secretary of the MSI of the province of Turin, which was set on fire.[18]

The BR took a new step with a qualitatively different action on 3 March 1972. That day, they carried out their first kidnapping, that of Idalgo Macchiarini, a SIT-Siemens executive responsible for production. It was Moretti who proposed this action which he organised and achieved.[19] Macchiarini was kidnapped in Milan by four brigadists who were wearing balaclavas, then he was detained for about 20 minutes in a Fiat 850 van, where he underwent a quick trial by a 'mobile people's court'.[20] He was mostly pictured with the barrel of a Walther P38 resting on his cheek and his gaze fixed on another pistol. A sign hung around his neck warning: 'Red Brigades. Hit and run! Nothing will go unpunished. Hit one to educate a hundred! All power to the armed people!'[21]He was finally released with a leaflet which defined him as 'a typical neo-fascist, a neo-fascist in a white shirt who is the black shirt of our time'.[22]

The event received considerable echo as the social climate remained violent. On 11 March 1972, clashes took place in Milan between the police and leftist demonstrators who tried to prevent an MSI meeting from taking place. Molotov cocktails were thrown at the *Corriere della Sera* newspaper building, considered the spokesperson for the Right. Two days later, on 13 March, the deputy secretary of the section of the MSI of Cesano Boscone was beaten and photographed by five brigadists.[23] A few days later, on 15 March, Feltrinelli's body was found under a high-voltage pylon in Segrate, near Milan, with a few explosive charges near it.

While the publisher's death caused some GAP activists to join the BR, the repression was also intensifying against the organisation which was now considered the most dangerous of the extra-parliamentary Left. A few days after the action against Cesano Boscone, 12 brigadists were arrested during a vast operation against the far-left. They were all accused of having participated in an armed gang. However, due to the legislation then in force, they were quickly released after a short period of preventive detention.[24]

The police then knew the BR's main leaders.[25] From 1971, the *Divizione Investigazioni Generali ed Operazioni Speciali* (General Investigations and Special Operations Division or DIGOS), the carabinieri and the secret services began to try to infiltrate the BR. Twenty years later, a general of the carabinieri explained that the security forces appealed for this mission to people recruited from outside, members of the security forces or 'terrorists whom we had caught and convinced to enter in the group'.[26]

DIGOS had an informant within the BR, Marco Pisetta, who had been involved in far-left actions since the days of the University of Trento when he met Curcio. While serving three years in prison for an attack that did not claim any casualties, he was recruited by police and released early to enter the BR. He provided a lot of information and even wrote a long document in which he described the BR organisation and gave the names of activists he knew.[27]

On 2 May 1972, police discovered BR bases in Milan, the main one of which was on Via Boiardo, and arrested 30 brigadists. It was Pisetta who gave the names and addresses that made this police success possible. But this operation missed its goal since the principal leaders, Cagol, Curcio, Franceschini, Morlacchi, Moretti and some others managed to flee. Investigators failed to keep the news of the operation secret, the results of which hit television news the same day. The awkwardness of the authorities was fraught with

Idalgo Macchiarini being held by *Brigate Rosse* gunmen. (Author's collection)

Margherita Cagol, in a photo from the early 1970s. (Albert Grandolini collection)

consequences. The BR had not been annihilated and their leaders went underground.[28]

The First BR Frameworks

After a few nights spent with a colleague from SIT-Siemens who did not belong to the BR, Moretti joined Morlacchi, Curcio, Cagol and Franceschini, who had found refuge in a farm in the Lodigiano region.[29] Curcio summed up the state of mind of the fleeing BR:

> The situation was decidedly grim: Feltrinelli is dead, the GAPs have practically disappeared, the French comrades of New Resistance, Andreas Baader, Ulrike Meinhof and the other German militants of the *Rote Armee Fraktion* (Red Army Faction or RAF) were almost all arrested. A reasonable assessment led us to believe that the experience of armed struggle in Europe had more or less failed and we only had to raise the oars when the time came.[30]

The feeling of discouragement that Curcio expressed did not last long. Faced with the police force's effectiveness, BR leaders understood that maintaining an open structure was a dangerous handicap. If the organisation wanted to continue to live, it had to restructure, compartmentalise itself and its members become professional revolutionaries.[31] They defined the new structures of the BR, divided into columns that brought together different factories or neighbourhood brigades, all compartmentalised so as not to compromise, in the event of arrest, the entire group.[32]

Measures were taken to improve the clandestinity, to filter new recruits more severely in order to protect themselves from infiltration, and to completely abandon semi-illegality. The underground militants, referred to as 'regular', began to receive a salary corresponding to that of a metallurgist. With the money collected from the robberies and thefts, the BR bought houses and apartments that were used to hide activists, to collect information to plan actions, and to store weapons. These were starting to be bought abroad, in Switzerland or Liechtenstein, in Italian armouries using false documents, or to be stolen.[33]

The 2 May police operation failed to destroy the BR. Many arrested activists were released after a few months in prison, while sympathisers and activists in the factories had not been affected by the arrests. The BR leaders were then divided into two groups. The first with Franceschini, Moretti and Morlacchi returned to Milan to form a column that developed in the districts of Lambrate, Quarto Oggiaro, Giambellino and the main factories, Pirelli, Siemens and Alfa Romeo. The second group with Curcio, Cagol and Ferrari settled in Turin and concentrated its action on the Fiat factories.[34] It was also seeking to develop within the other large Turin factories, to extend to those of Pininfarina, Singer and Lancia, even if Fiat remained at the centre of its concerns and actions.[35] The BR thus succeeded in recruiting new militants and increasing their influence. According to Curcio, they would bring together at that time 911 people.[36]

The conflict that broke out in September 1972 at Fiat with the occupation of the Mirafiori factory, a general strike and clashes between demonstrators and the police, lasted several months. A large demonstration in Turin on 25 November was violently repressed by the police and left 30 injured. In this context, the BR attracted the sympathy of many workers who did not hesitate to draw the five-pointed star in the workshops. Some joined the BR, for example Cristoforo Piancone, Luco Nicolotti, Angela Basone and Rocco Micaletto. It was around them that the Turin column developed, coming into action in the autumn. On 26 November, 11 Fiat executives' cars were set on fire and on 17 December, six cars belonging to members of the employers' union, two belonging to security guards and one belonging to an MSI activist were burnt.[37]

On 11 January 1973, nine brigadists from the Turin column attacked the provincial headquarters of the right-wing union *Confederazione Italiana Sindicati Nazionali dei Lavoratori* (Italian Confederation of National Trade Unions or CISNAL) in Turin, which they devastated by beating those present. This action aimed to protest against the MSI congress which was to be held in Rome in mid-January. It also took place the day before violent clashes between police force and workers occupying the Lancia factory in Chivasso. On the 13th, in Milan, police attacked a group of students in front of the university and seriously injured a young man who died a few days later.[38]

In this dramatic climate of conflict, on the morning of 12 February 1973, in Turin, the BR kidnapped CISNAL secretary Bruno Labate as he left his home.[39] He was interrogated for a few hours, his hair was shaved, and he was brought back almost naked the next day to the door of the Fiat factory in Mirafiori in a car with Curcio, Cagol, Buonavita and Ferrari. The latter handcuffed their prisoner to a lamp post, leaving a leaflet around his neck and left the premises.[40] A little over two weeks after this kidnapping, on 28 February, the workers' struggle resumed at Fiat and lasted until 2 April. The BR present in the factory participated in the movement and their influence was growing.[41]

In Milan, the BR's capacity for action was comparable to that of the Turin column. On 15 January 1973, three members of the Milanese column, armed with submachine guns and pistols, took over the premises of the Union of Christian Entrepreneurs, locked the secretary in the bathroom and stole confidential documents.[42] They continued their armed propaganda campaign with the kidnapping of Alfa Romeo leader Michele Mincuzzi in Milan on 28 June. This action followed the same scenario as that of Macchiarini. Mincuzzi came face to face with a commando team as he got out of his car. After a brief struggle, he was pushed into a van and driven into the countryside. He was interrogated in a van and then released in Arese with a leaflet around his neck that described him as 'A fascist leader of Alfa Romeo, on trial by the BR.' The PCI used this action to condemn the BR which it described as an 'organisation of bandits which acts with delinquent methods and whose aim is to fuel the strategy of tension. On the small card board is drawn a red star which does not have five points, but six; this is the Star of David. The perpetrators of this criminal enterprise confused a communist symbol with an Israeli symbol.' This was actually an error by Moretti that had no significance for the understanding of the phenomenon.[43]

However, the BR quickly disappeared from the news in the face of two events that resonated widely in Italy, the coup in Chile and the Yom Kippur War. The fall of Allende prompted the PCI secretary, Enrico Berlinguer, to propose a historic compromise between the Left and the DC that would result in the creation of a grand coalition bringing together the democratic parties. He thus wanted to prevent his country from a political evolution of the Chilean type.[44] The conflict between Israel and the Arab countries, for its part, caused an energy and economic crisis which revived social unrest but also laid the foundations for Western deindustrialisation. Added to these events was the resurgence of neo-fascist terrorism. In 1972, in Peteano, in the province of Gorizia, a car stuffed with TNT killed three carabinieri. In Milan, on 17 May 1973, during a ceremony in the presence of the President of the Council, Mariano Rumor, a bomb was launched which left four dead and 52 wounded.[45] These two attacks were the work of far-right activists.

The Amerio Kidnapping

The context of intense social struggles and neo-fascist attacks seemed to confirm the political analysis of the BR who feared the preparation of an 'informal coup', similar to that experienced in France in 1958. The BR seemed to believe then that the whole proletariat, as a class, felt a climate of repression in the same way as the revolutionary Left. This entirely ideological and false analysis certainly prompted them to step up their action.

This turning point was expressed with the kidnapping of Ettore Amerio, a top executive of the Fiat company, on 10 December 1973, an action which took place in the context of tension caused by the oil crisis and the dismissal of 300 workers by Fiat. The operation was being carried out by a commando group disguised as workers from the SIP telephone company led by Ferrari. Amerio had no time to react and found himself locked in a van followed by a red Fiat 124 which took him to a 'people's prison'.[46] For the first time, instead of keeping their hostage for a few hours, the BR sequestered him for eight days while leading an intense propaganda activity in Turin, Genoa – where Rocco Micaletto was forming a column – and in Milan. The BR distributed leaflets in various factories in Milan but also in Genoa, Arese, Piacenza and Modena. At the gates of the SIT-Siemens and Breda factories in Porto Marghera, two cars with loudspeakers broadcasted BR releases accompanied by revolutionary songs.

For a few days, Turin was put under a state of siege. Police patrolled the working-class neighbourhoods while helicopters flew over the city, connected by radio with the police on the ground. The Feltrinelli family's country residence was even searched.[47] Fiat finally declared that it did not want to resort to redundancies and on 18 December Amerio was released carrying a leaflet: 'He collaborated satisfactorily. Amerio's imprisonment demonstrated that it is not us who should be afraid. On the contrary, we must arm ourselves and accept war, because winning is possible.'[48] If the length of sequestration was unprecedented, the release of the hostage without consideration showed that the BR were still in a logic of intimidation and that they were putting limits on their use of force.

By the end of 1973, the BR enjoyed a certain aura of romanticism and general sympathy among the workers who appreciated their competence in the problems of the factory, their quick and efficient methods and their limited use of violence. This allowed them to start settling in Veneto, especially in the petrochemical sector of Marghera, in Mestre, in the Breda shipyards and in the University of Padua. In the Venetian region, a first brigadist experience took place in 1970 with the formation of the Ferretto Brigade which included members of the extra-parliamentary Left and those close to the BR such as Giorgio Semeria. At the beginning of 1974, the BR sent Fabrizio Pelli, Ognibene and Micaletto to the region, who came into contact with Carlo Picchiura, Susanna Ronconi and Nadia Mantovani of the Ferretto Brigade. Finally, the BR absorbed the latter to give birth to a new column, made up of a few militants in Mestre, Padua, Treviso and Venice.[49]

In this phase of BR's geographic development, the organisation retained a still rudimentary structure. While until the end of 1972, it only existed in Milan, the installation of a column in Turin in 1973, then its extension in Veneto and the Marche province, where a revolutionary committee was formed in 1974, did not lead to the creation of a real centralised management structure but only of a coordinating body called the *Nazionale* made up of Curcio, Cagol, Franceschini, Moretti and Morlacchi.[50]

It was in this context of growing organisation, of the success of Amerio's kidnapping and of implantation in the factories that the BR appeared on the Italian national scene, challenging the state.

Ettore Amerio, in a release by the *Brigate Rosse* following his kidnapping. (Albert Grandolini collection)

4
THE END OF THE HISTORIC NUCLEUS, 1974–1975

The year 1974 was a pivotal year in the history of the BR, as would be the year 1978. Until then, armed propaganda was limited to a moderate level of violence and blood had never been shed. At a European level, the BR were then closer to the French *Gauche prolétarienne* (Proletarian Left or GP) than to the West German RAF. In 1974, their fate began to shift towards the German model of armed struggle when the French voluntarily laid down their arms. This choice carried a high price, the disappearance of the historical nucleus of the BR's founders.

The Sossi Kidnapping

At the beginning of 1974, the actions of BR multiplied. The armed propaganda directed to the workers continued with the burning of a car belonging to a director of SIT-Siemens on 16 January, followed by that of the director of personnel of Pirelli Bicocca a week later. On 13 February, the cars of some petrochemical executives in Marghera were set on fire and on 3 March, during a raid on the CISNAL provincial headquarters in Mestre, documents and files were taken away. On 27 March, the manager of Singer's car was burnt and on

9 April that of Breda-Fucine's manager in Sesto San Giovanni.[1] The emergence of more political targets aimed at the repressive state apparatus marked the emergence of a new direction. The BR, by launching Operation Girasole, were thus attempting to leave the field of factories and raised the level of armed struggle.

The deputy prosecutor of the Republic of Genoa, Mario Sossi was kidnapped by a commando on 18 April 1974. Sossi, a right-wing magistrate, was the prosecutor in the trial of the members of the *XXII Ottobre* group who sentenced Mario Rossi to life imprisonment. The BR had never acted in Genoa where they only had a base and a few militants. The operation began in 1973 when three regulars were sent to Genoa to establish the organisation there. All leaders, Cagol, Curcio, Ferrari, Bonavita, Bertolazzi, Ognibene, Pelli and Franceschini eventually travelled to the town to participate in the operation. The Turin column was responsible for preparing the kidnapping. Buovanita and Maurizio Ferrari watched the target, and followed the bus he took to go from his work in the Palace of Justice to his home in Albaro, studied his schedules, habits and routes, and collected any information about him.[2]

The operation mobilised many activists who were divided into three cells, each responsible for one of the phases of the kidnapping. A first cell, led by Cagol and Franceschini, had the mission of capturing Sossi (who was not accompanied by a police escort), a second to transport him to the holding place and a third which was responsible for monitoring and controlling him.

The commandos went into action on the evening of 18 April and waited for Sossi outside his house at around 8:00 p.m. The 18 brigadists were dispersed in the area where the kidnapping was to take place. Six carried out the physical capture of Sossi, three others ensured the transport of the hostage to his holding place and the nine others were in the neighbourhood, ready to intervene if necessary.[3] As he got off the bus, Sossi was followed by Buonavita, Ognibene and Semeria while three other brigadists were a little further away, in support. Semeria silenced the janitor while Buonavita and Ognibene threatened Sossi with their weapons. A van then arrived at full speed with Ferrari and Marra, and the prisoner climbed inside.[4] After a short drive, he was transferred, hidden in a bag, to an Autobianchi A112 driven by Franceschini and Bertolazzi. The car, preceded by a Fiat 128, driven by Cagol, took Via dell'Appennino along a road under construction which joined, after a few kilometres, the national road. After a short stretch on this road, they took less travelled roads to reach Tortona.[5]

The operation did not go smoothly. As they left Genoa with the hostage locked in a burlap bag, the second cell faced a roadblock. The Autobianchi carrying the prisoner cleared the checkpoint, but its passengers were convinced that Cagol's escort car had been stopped. In reality, Cagol had also passed without problem and tried to catch up with them, but his comrades, convinced that they were being pursued by the carabinieri, ambushed her and her car was hit by two bullets. It was only thanks to chance and Cagol's presence of mind that the operation did not end in fiasco.[6] Finally, the commando arrived in a house on the Sarezzano national road, in the province of Alessandria, a few kilometres from Tortona where, in a room on the upper floor, a large cube of wood soundproofed with polystyrene was installed which served as the hostage's cell. It was guarded by Franceschini, Bertolazzi and Cagol while Moretti and Curcio occupied another recently purchased farm, the Spiotta di Arzello farm, in Acqui Terme.[7]

The police immediately mobilised to find Judge Sossi. The commissioner of Genoa, Antonino Sciaraffa, swept the districts of the city and set up roadblocks. About 4,000 police officers, armed

Mario Sossi, photographed by the BR for propaganda purposes. (Albert Grandolini collection)

with machine guns, were mobilised.[8] According to some authors, the authorities knew a lot about Sossi's kidnapping and claim that the Interior Ministry's Reserved Affairs Office had an agent undercover in the BR, Francesco Marra. The latter was said to be a former neo-fascist parachutist who trained in Tuscany and Sardinia in the use of weapons before joining the BR.[9] Thanks to Marra, the head of the *Servizio Informazioni Difesa* (Defence Information Service or SID), General Vito Miceli would have known that the brigadists were going to kidnap Sossi, but he strangely did nothing to stop them. He then allegedly organised a meeting with his close associates to launch an armed operation to release the judge, suggesting that he knew the location of his 'people's prison'. But these subordinates feared that such an operation would end in carnage in which the hostage could be killed, and the idea was reportedly abandoned. However, there is no evidence for the existence of Miceli's plan except for the testimony of General Gianadelio Maletti. Then there was only Franceschini, Bertolazzi and Cagol who knew the location where Sossi was imprisoned, not even Curcio and Moretti, and even less so Marra.[10] Above all, there is no material evidence that the latter was an infiltrator, which had been confirmed by the former Minister of the Interior Paolo Emilio Taviani and by General Dalla Chiesa.[11]

On 25 April, a press release signed by the GAP of Genoa stated, 'Comrades of the BR, for the executioners and the oppressors there is no need for trial. This is why we ask that the only slogan be: outside Rossi or death in Sossi.' The next day, the BR demanded 'the release of all fellow political prisoners' in exchange for the release the judge.[12] On 5 May, a new BR declaration called for eight imprisoned members of the *XXII Ottobre* group to be released and sent to Cuba, North Korea or Algeria.[13] They increased their pressure on 2 May by attacking the offices of Edgardo Sogno of the Democratic Resistance Committee in Milan and those of the Centro Sturzo in Turin.[14]

The days of 9 to 13 May were particularly dramatic. On 9 May, a revolt broke out among the inmates of Alessandria Prison, near Genoa. The carabinieri's assault regained control of the prison but at the cost of the lives of seven people, including five hostages, while 14 were wounded. For the BR, this repression was interpreted as a sign of the firmness of the state.[15]

Victims of the bombing of the Piazza della Loggia, in Padua, during an anti-fascist demonstration on 29 May 1974. (Albert Grandolini collection)

To break the deadlock, on 18 May, the BR announced that they had sentenced Sossi to death. On the 20th, the Genoa Court of Appeal granted the provisional release of the nine prisoners of the *XXII Ottobre* group. The decision was the subject of considerable controversy. On 21 May, Prime Minister Rumor, a supporter of firmness, condemned it. That same day, the BR again guaranteed Sossi's release if the prisoners were granted provisional release and found refuge at the Cuban Embassy in the Vatican. But the prosecutor of Genoa, Francesco Coco, decided to challenge the decision of the Court of Appeal before the Supreme Court and therefore to block it.[16] According to Franceschini, the PCI also played a role in this episode by lobbying to derail negotiations with the Cuban embassy to grant prisoners political asylum on the Caribbean island.[17]

The BR then chose not to implement their threat of execution of the hostage. On 22 May, Sossi was released and gave an interview to *Corriere della Sera* that complemented the organisation's propaganda success. The judge explained in fact that the brigadists were 'very organised', 'well documented' and above all 'very numerous'.[18] On the day Sossi's interview was published, a neo-fascist attack took place in Brescia killing and injuring several people during an anti-fascist protest. The attack, immediately attributed to the far-right, contrasted, in the eyes of public opinion, with that of the BR who had released Sossi unharmed.[19]

Despite its outcome, the kidnapping of magistrate Sossi was the first BR action to have an impact on the country's political life. Operation Girasole forced the authorities to enter into negotiations with the BR, and above all it showed the weakness of a divided state where the political power was opposed to the judicial power on the issue of the release of political prisoners, without forgetting controversies between magistrates and police officials accusing each other of incompetence.[20] From the point of view of the authorities', the BR now appeared to be a growing and formidable threat that had to be eradicated as quickly as possible.

The First Deaths

On 17 June 1974, at the MSI headquarters on Via Zabarella in Padua, two neo-fascist activists, Giuseppe Mazzola and Graziano Giralucci, were found dead. The two victims were each found lying on the ground, tied up with a bullet to the back of the head. As the press reported internal far-right feuds, a BR statement claimed the action: 'An armed group of the Red Brigades has occupied the MSI headquarters in Padua. The two fascists present, having reacted violently, were executed.'[21]

The BR had recently established themselves in Veneto, in particular in Porto Marghera within the Montedison factory. The main activists were then Pelli and Gallinari who joined the organisation in 1973.[22] Curcio would later recount that the BR of Veneto autonomously decided to enter the MSI premises in Padua to search for documents related to the Brescia bombing.[23] The operation was ill-prepared and turned into a fiasco.

The commando was composed of Martino Serafino, Giorgio Semeria, Susanna Ronconi, Roberto Ognibene and Fabrizio Pelli. The plan of action was simple, two brigadists had to neutralise the people present in the room and two others searched and took away any interesting documents. In the preceding days, Ronconi and Serafino led the preparatory observation, spying on the activity of the section, while Ognibene pretended that he wanted to join the MSI and took the opportunity to enter the premises and inspect them. On the morning of the action, Pelli and Ognibene entered the room and found two MSI activists whom they forced to kneel down at gunpoint. When they began to tie their hands, the two men reacted, and a struggle began which ended with gunshots; the two neo-fascists had each been killed by a gunshot to the back of the neck.[24]

The BR's national leadership was informed in the following days. Should it claim a murderous action that had not been decided by the leaders? The temptation not to was great, but finally the BR decided to claim it. To explain this choice, Curcio argued that the organisation did not want his involvement to be discovered at a later date.[25] The BR also certainly took into account that part of the Left approved of and justified action against fascists accused of massacring the population. Curcio nevertheless pointed out that the idea of killing at that time was not an objective of the BR: 'death was not part of the political objectives of the time, even if it was not excluded a priori that during our actions exchanges of fire are possible.'[26]

The attack on the MSI headquarters in Padua took place in a special context. The neo-fascists reviving the strategy of tension were organising new massacres. On 19 May 1974, in Brescia,

One of 8 fatalities and 94 wounded of the Piazza della Loggia bombing. (Albert Grandolini collection)

a young right-wing extremist, Silvio Ferrari, was killed while transporting a bomb in Piazza del Mercato. A 7.65mm pistol with two magazines was found near the body. In the same city, on 29 May, a bomb exploded in Piazza della Loggia during an anti-fascist demonstration leaving eight dead and 94 wounded.[27] On 4 August, aboard the Italicus train, a high-explosive bomb detonated in a tunnel between Bologna and Florence, killing 12 and injuring 105.[28] These slaughters dampened the echo of the deaths in Padua.

After this episode, the BR nevertheless suspended their activities in Veneto for a while. The column was dissolved, replaced by a territorial committee made up of a few militants organised between Mestre, Padua, Treviso and Venice. It would not be operational again until a few years later, when it was reorganised by Nadia Ponti and Vincenzo Guagliardo.[29]

The BR Settles in Rome

At the end of 1974, the BR again discussed the structures of the organisation and the need to adapt them in the face of police offensives. After the arrests of May 1972, they equipped themselves with an agile organisation capable of resisting repression. The columns had become organisationally autonomous and, in order to coordinate their actions with the national strategic orientation, fronts were formed with the aim of centralising the different aspects of the BR's activities. A Logistics Front was thus responsible for the search for weapons, bases, licence plates and the falsification of documents, while a Factory Front coordinated actions in this sector. The whole was headed by a new central body, the *Comitato Esecutivo* (Executive Committee or CE) responsible for directing and coordinating all the activities of the fronts and the columns. Alongside this CE, the *Direzione Strategica* (Strategic Direction or DS) replaced the *Nazionale* to determine the strategy of the entire organisation.

As the BR perfected their structures, they also decided to settle in Rome as close as possible to the 'heart of the state'. In order to organise a Roman column and to study possible objectives, Franceschini was sent to the capital with Pelli and Gallinari where they met activists from the districts of Tiburtino and Garbatella. Franceschini then began to consider organising a sensational action, the kidnapping of a prestigious politician like Andreotti. He discussed it with Moretti, Curcio and Cagol because he believed that this operation would be easy to achieve. Roman politicians then moved without armed escort while the Italian capital itself had not yet become a safe city.[30]

The situation seemed favourable to the BR. The proximity between certain sectors of the secret services and the armed forces

A wrecked carriage of the Italicus train, bombed by Italian Neo-Nazis on 4 August 1974. (Albert Grandolini collection)

with right-wing extremists forced the government to intervene. In December 1970, the coup led by the fascist Junio Valerio Borghese, who had occupied the Interior Ministry for several hours, took place, according to some, under the eyes of the SID and the American embassy.[31] On 15 July 1974, Andreotti, Minister of Defence, had to dismiss a dozen generals and admirals in order to prevent a new coup, scheduled for 10 August. On 4 August, almost in response to this act, the Italicus train attack took place. On 6 August, still near Bologna, 18kg of explosives were discovered by police at the entrance to a railway tunnel. Finally, on 23 August, the Turin Court of Justice discovered the proposed 'White Coup' organised by Edgardo Sogno, Randolfo Pacciardi and Luigi Cavallo, the aim of which was to create a presidential republic, thanks to the intervention of the armed forces.[32] If the state finally decided to strike against the Right, it was also forging the instrument that would put the BR out of harm's way.

Dalla Chiesa and the Special Counterterrorism Nuclei

Operation Girasole was a shock to the state, demonstrating the maturity of the BR who managed to kidnap and detain a senior official for 35 days. An Appeals Court even bowed to their demands against the will of the government. The Sossi kidnapping therefore marked a turning point in the state's assessment of the BR. With the exception of the arrests of 1972, they were able to function without much opposition from the police. The brigadists were partly known to the police and the magistrates but had not been actively prosecuted. Milan Police Commissioner Antonino Allegra later confirmed that 'undoubtedly not everything has been done [against the BR] which should have been'.[33] In the Chamber of Deputies, therefore, the pressure was increasing on the government to put an end to the organisation's activities.

In the months that followed, the pursuit of the BR by police forces became more intense. On 22 May, on the eve of Sossi's liberation, a carabinieri unit specialising in the fight against terrorism was formed in Turin, under the orders of General Carlo Alberto Dalla Chiesa. The latter had been, since October 1973, commander of the 1st Carabinieri Brigade of Turin after having spent several years in Palermo. Its jurisdiction extended over Piedmont, Liguria and the Aosta Valley, an area where the BR were active. During the Sossi kidnapping, he proposed to the Interior Ministry to create a unit solely responsible for this case.[34] The *Nucleo Speciale Antiterrorismo* (Special Counterterrorism Unit or NSA) thus created included seven carabinieri officers and 33 non-commissioned officers as well as a dozen men from the judicial police or the secret services.[35]

The initiative for the NSA's creation was therefore led by the Minister of the Interior Taviani, who thus wished to train a new generation of more modern and efficient investigators. On 1 June, he also created another body, the General Inspectorate for the Fight against Terrorism under the leadership of Commissioner Emilio Santillo, responsible for coordinating operational information and security interventions across the country.[36] While this service quickly faced many problems, the NSA achieved a series of successes within a few months.

So far, each BR action had been investigated separately, without the authorities seeking to establish links between them or exchange information. Dalla Chiesa, on the contrary, believed that it was necessary to have a centralised and specialist approach and wished to investigate the organisation as a whole, as he had in Sicily with the Mafia. For this, he had a small group of men enjoying a certain freedom of action so that the unit was mobile and flexible, able to act in any country to collect, analyse and to centrally interpret the information collected. He also used police techniques against

General Carlo Alberto Dalla Chiesa, the head of the Italian counter-terrorism effort in the 1970s. (Albert Grandolini collection)

organised crime, which he perfected in the fight against the BR. Dalla Chiesa's methods were particularly innovative for this time. He thus revolutionised the way in which police investigations were carried out in Italy and these innovations would be repeated later in France and West Germany.[37]

Dalla Chiesa began by trying to understand who the BR were and their environment. The carabinieri therefore directed their investigations towards the study and analysis of the BR's documentation in order to better determine their strategic objectives and to conduct adequate mapping of their internal structure. They were also interested in radical Left circles which could serve as logistical support and a reservoir of sympathisers. An example of the NSA's methods was the careful study of land registers in Milan, Turin and other cities to identify houses and apartments that the BR bought with false documents. They thus succeeded in discovering 38 bases in Milan, Turin, Piacenza, Pavia and Rome up to May 1978, where they seized large quantities of equipment and arrested 152 brigadists.[38]

The centralisation of information also showed its effectiveness. Thus, the carabinieri of Pianello Val Tidone near Piacenza inspected a damaged and empty house where they found documents with the BR's signature. The information was passed on to Dalla Chiesa's unit, which launched a full investigation. The confiscated material led to a series of arrests between Milan and Piacenza. A number of them were suspected of being involved in the Sossi kidnapping. In addition, on the basis of the clues found, two other bases were located, one in Milan and the other in a neighbouring village, Robbiano di Mediglia.[39] In addition to the information provided by the local authorities, the NSA also received help from the PCI, which began a long collaboration by providing it with a lot of information.[40]

Pinerolo

The NSA got quick results. On 27 May 1974, an illegal brigatist, Paolo Maurizio Ferrari, was arrested in Florence during a search.[41] On 7 June, in San Nicola Arcella, carabinieri discovered the house where the BR had taken refuge in May 1972. They used the material discovered to arrest Adriano Carnelutti on 7 July. Then Giorgio

Spiotta d'Arzello farm, seen after it was discovered by the Italian security services. (Author's collection)

Curcio and Franceschini's arrest in Pinerolo. (Albert Grandolini collection)

of this former Franciscan priest appeared in certain Italian newspapers which devoted articles to him presenting him as a 'communist guerrilla'. Girotto returned to Italy with letters from the leaders of the Cuban Communist Party in which they attested that he was trained in guerrilla warfare. He also claimed to have had relations with the Uruguayan Tupamaros. He came into contact with the BR through lawyer Giambattista Lazagna. After some hesitation, the organisation leadership decided to meet with him. During the first meeting, Curcio appreciated his motivations. During the second, the latter and Moretti suggested that he entered into the organisation to train the militants in urban guerrilla warfare, notably at the Spiotta farm near Asti.[44]

The BR finally decided that Curcio should meet Girotto in Pinerolo, near Turin, on 8 September to drive him to the Spiotta farm, where he would stay for some time before joining the Logistics Front. Moretti and Franceschini were informed of this decision on Saturday 7 September during a meeting in Parma. At the end of it, Moretti returned to Milan while Franceschini, who should have left for Rome, stayed with Curcio. The next day, in violation of the organisation rules, the two went to Pinerolo.

It was in this context that a mysterious event occurred. The day before, a phone call was received by the wife of lawyer Arrigo Levati – a BR supporter – that alerted the organisation to the risks of Curcio's arrest. According to some, those who placed the call were agents of the Mossad, the Israeli secret service which would have liked to protect an organisation opposed to an Italian government which pursued a pro-Arab foreign policy. Moretti and Peci's statements asserted that in 1974 the Mossad offered weapons and money to the BR and also provided them with the address of the hiding place of the 'traitor' Pisetta, who was put into shelter in West Germany by the Italian police, give some credibility to this hypothesis.[45] However, it is more

Pinotti, Pietro Sabatino, Francesco Cattaneo and Paolo Gastaldi were also arrested.[42]

As in his fight against the Mafia, Dalla Chiesa knew that infiltration was the best way to strike the BR leadership. But he knew this type of operation was tricky. Nevertheless, he found the ideal candidate: Silvano Girotto.[43] During the Sossi kidnapping, the name likely that this 'leak' was the work of carabinieri, or even members of the Interior Ministry, hostile to Dalla Chiesa.[46]

Following this phone call, Moretti, who returned to Milan, was tasked with trying to find Curcio before the meeting with Girotto. He tried to contact him in Parma but he had already left the city with Franceschini. He also failed to make contact with Cagol, Curcio's wife. He then summoned a group of activists to watch the streets of the city and Pinerolo area in order to warn the latter of the danger. Curcio was still nowhere to be found, because he took the precaution of driving on minor roads.[47]

There are many hypotheses about the reasons for Moretti's failure to find Curcio. According to some, a few days earlier, in Parma, a meeting of the BR's leaders was held in which it was decided to oust Moretti from the CE because of his intransigence in the negotiations for the release of Sossi.[48] From this fact, writers quickly draw the conclusion that Moretti deliberately did not find Curcio and Franceschini. Admittedly, Moretti may have deliberately avoided warning them out of resentment against the decision to expel him from the CE. Other authors go further and advance the hypothesis that Moretti was manipulated and intentionally set free. To support this thesis, they argue that if the carabinieri had waited a while, they could have arrested Moretti as well. The conclusion they draw from these conjectures was that the latter was deliberately set free so that he could take the leadership of the BR and impose his strategy which would have served the interests of certain sectors of the state apparatus.

Curcio refutes this idea and gives another explanation for Moretti's non-arrest. He says that at the time of the meeting in Parma, he was working with Franceschini on the drafting of a brochure based on the documents stolen from Edgardo Sogno's office and concerning the coup prepared by the latter with the complicity of politicians and senior officials. This documentation would have fallen into the hands of the carabinieri at the time of his arrest with Franceschini. Years later, during the Turin trial, he asked the judge to make them public, but the magistrate replied that they had disappeared. According to Curcio, the arrest of Pinerolo by the carabinieri was triggered because they knew the enormous sensitivity of these documents and wanted to recover them at all costs, even that of letting Moretti escape.[49]

Regarding the idea that Moretti would have taken advantage of this episode to rise to the leadership of the BR, Ognibene demonstrates its inconsistency:

> The truth is that there was a great political difference between the revolutionary path that Renato, Alberto and Mara had in mind and that of Moretti who, on the contrary, had a much more militarist conception of the BR. Of course, after this arrest, the BR changed their face. But not immediately, because Mara Cagol was free. She and most of the underground comrades were in favour of the line dictated by Curcio and Franceschini. Only a small minority agreed with Moretti who, moreover, always accepted the decisions of the majority … The carabinieri knew that at the scene of the arrest there would only be Curcio. Alberto and Mara would remain free and thought differently from Moretti. So, nothing would have changed.[50]

A simple examination of the unfolding of this episode is enough to show that the charges against Moretti are highly questionable and rather aim to conceal the responsibility of Curcio and Franceschini in their arrest. Curcio should not have left Parma without telling anyone, and Franceschini should not have accompanied him to Pinerolo. The two leaders did not abide by their organisation's own safety rules. Only Curcio was to meet Girotto, so the carabinieri could only hope to arrest him and not other members of the BR leadership.[51] Finally, on a small side road near Pinerolo, Curcio and Franceschini's Fiat 128 was stopped behind a van at a level crossing. Cars arrived behind it from which exited carabinieri in civilian clothes who pointed pistols at the two brigadist leaders and handcuffed them in a few seconds.[52]

With Curcio and Franceschini in the hands of the police, the DS met at the Spiotta farm on 13 October and decided to appoint Lauro Azzolini and Franco Bonisoli to the direction of the Milanese column, while Cagol remained in Turin. The next day, however, another blow was dealt to the organisation by Dalla Chiesa. The latter discovered a BR base in Robbiano di Mediglia near Milan and set up a trap there. Pietro Bassi, who was unaware of the discovery of the base, was arrested there on 14 October. The next day, Ognibene also went there. He smelt the trap and killed a carabiniere, but he was injured and arrested.[53] The NSA investigations continued and on 30 October in Turin, Gallinari and Buonavita were arrested.[54] In February of the following year, Morlacchi was also arrested in Switzerland.[55]

Between late 1974 and early 1975, the BR suffered a series of notable arrests that brought the organisation to the brink of collapse. At the end of 1974, the survivors were reduced to launching minor actions such as the burning of cars in Turin, Pavia and Veneto.[56] The economic crisis that was beginning to hit Italy was nevertheless allowing them to recover and rebuild their strength.

The 1975 Strategic Resolution

In 1975, Italy entered an economic crisis. The country experienced a recession that year with gross domestic product at -3.7 percent and inflation at 17 percent. To cope with this deterioration, the companies, particularly in the automotive sector, were preparing restructuring plans which resulted in the automation of production chains and the dismissal of many workers. In the autumn of 1974, major layoffs had taken place at the Fiat and Lancia companies, which sparked social movements, including strikes and demonstrations in factories. On 25 November, the BR took part in this movement by burning the cars of five Fiat executives and the next day they attacked a member of staff. This action generated some approval within Fiat's Mirafiori plant, but company management and the *Sindacato Italiano dell'Automobile* (Italian Automobile Union or SIDA) finally signed an agreement on 5 December. In response, the BR burst into two SIDA offices in Mirafiori and Rivalta on 11 December, briefly sequestering two employees.

At the beginning of 1975, Fiat announced the need for a restructuring of the company which would result in the partial unemployment of thousands of workers. In response, new strikes and factory occupations began and one that started on 22 April in Mirafiori continued into May and June. The BR did not stay away from the workers' protests and, on 19 June in Turin, they injured an assistant foreman at the Fiat factory in Rivalta. They also resumed the offensive in the Milanese factories. Despite these actions, during the first six months of 1975, 6,000 workers were dismissed and 71,552 were placed on technical unemployment.[57]

In April 1975, the DS drew up a Resolution which offered an analysis which, in retrospect, seemed quite relevant to the transformations of capitalism underway in Italy. According to them, the process of capitalist restructuring was a global phenomenon which profoundly transformed the relation of production in order to cancel out the gains obtained by the workers' movement. The

BR therefore foresaw the long period leading up to the end of the century, which saw capitalism move production sites at will, restructuring and markets in which the labour force cost less and was less unionised and politicised. This new economic globalisation that they announced, allowed the BR to introduce into their analysis the notion of the imperialist state of multinationals. For them, the responsibility for the exploitation of the working class no longer rested only on national industrial groups, but on an international system of domination of capital led by multinationals protected by the United States and financed by the contribution made by each government belonging to the Western bloc. In this new system, the Italian state became the instrument of the imperialist bourgeoisie in its enterprise of exploiting the weakest social strata and therefore a prime target for the BR.[58]

A demonstration on the streets of Milano, in April 1975. (Albert Grandolini collection)

A left-wing demonstrator killed by police during demonstrations in Torino, on 17 April 1975. (Albert Grandolini collection)

On the strategic level, the Resolution affirmed that despite the political crisis, the regime was still strong while the revolutionary forces were weak. In this situation, the armed propaganda retained its correctness by striking the adversary directly while allowing the workers' movement to strengthen itself and prepare for the civil war which would be the epilogue of the struggle between the proletariat and the Italian state. On the tactical level, the BR then set themselves the objective of freeing the militants in prison, the offensive in the factories and the attack against the state, in particular the DC Party.[59]

Regarding the first point, during the winter, the DS met in Veneto and decided, on Cagol's proposal, to attack the prison of Casale Monferrato where Curcio was being held. On 18 February 1975 at 4:10 p.m., while Cagol reported to the prison under the pretext of delivering a package to a prisoner, a commando group infiltrated the building. In a few minutes, and without firing a shot, the BR managed to free the prisoner.[60] At that time the general condition of Italian prisons was so deplorable that General Dalla Chiesa demanded, shortly after, the creation of maximum security prisons or 'special prisons'.[61] Curcio, freed, became the director of the column of Milan, while Cagol was named at the head of that of Turin and Moretti was sent to Rome to try to form another.[62]

Cagol's Death

The Italian situation at the beginning of 1975 was particularly troubled. In addition to strikes and factory occupations, the months of March and April were marked by a series of clashes between young people from the Right and the Left but also against the police forces which left many injured and some dead.[63]

Despite this troubled climate, police forces continued to hit the BR. On 2 May 1975, they discovered a base in Turin and the next day they arrested Arialdo Lintrami and Tonino Paroli, seizing many notes and weapons. In response, on 15 May, the BR attacked the

Mara Cagol's body after the firefight with Carabinieri on 5 June 1975. (Open source)

Another view of the same scene, with Cagol's body meanwhile covered by a blanket. (Open source)

headquarters of a conservative organisation linked to DC member Massimo De Carolis in Milan. During the action, De Carolis was gagged, subjected to a 'proletarian trial' and shot in the legs.[64] This was the first time that the BR used this new method of aggression, called in Italian '*gambizzazioni*' which marked an escalation in the violence inflicted by the organisation, since if it was not fatal, it left the victim disabled for life.[65]

In order to finance the organisation, the BR decided to kidnap the Piedmontese industrialist Vittorio Vallarino Garcia and to set him free only in exchange for ransom. The action was carried out on 4 June by Moretti and four other activists, and the prisoner was transported to the Spiotta farm in the hills of Acqui Terme.[66] However, during the operation, Massimo Maraschi, who was part of the support group, was involved in an accident. Arrested and taken to a carabinieri barracks, he was found in possession of a 7.65mm pistol and false documents, triggering a series of checks in isolated places in the region.[67]

The next day, 5 June, Lieutenant Umberto Rocca, commander of the Acqui Carabinieri company, arrived at the Spiotta farm with Major Rosario Cattafi, commander of the post of Acqui Terme, and the carabinieri Giovanni D'Alfonso and Pietro Barberis. The farm, bought in 1973 by Cagol under the name Marta Caruso, was among the suspicious real estate transactions spotted by Dalla Chiesa's men.[68] The carabinieri, after inspecting the cars present, requested reinforcements from the operations centre and surrounded the farm. Inside the house were the hostage, Cagol, and an unknown brigadist who, after inviting the carabinieri to enter, threw an SRCM hand grenade. Rocca was seriously injured in the eye and left arm, while Cattafi, also hit, retaliated. Cagol – injured in the arm – and the unknown brigadist, attempted to escape and they injured D'Alfonso with their M1 pistols. They got into their car but had to stop in front of the carabinieri car which blocked the path leading to the main road. Cagol and her companion preferred to surrender to the carabiniere Barberis. According to Barberis, Cagol got out of the car raising her hands, but her comrade took a grenade from his pocket and threw it at Barberis before fleeing. The carabiniere threw himself forward and opened fire, killing Cagol. After a few minutes, reinforcements arrived and freed Garcia. According to the brigadist who fled, Cagol had in fact remained seated on the ground with her arms raised. After a few minutes of continuing to run, he heard gunshots, suggesting that Cagol had been executed.[69]

For the BR, the operation was a disaster. They lost a very experienced leader and a carabiniere was killed in an action that did not originally involve the use of weapons. It also showed the operational weakness of the BR who had only two militants to watch their hostage and ensure the security of the farm. The carabinieri did not stop at this success. A few days later, they discovered another BR base in Baranzate di Bollate near Milan and arrested two other members of the CE, Pierluigi Zuffada and Attilio Casaletti.[70]

Despite these many successes, in July 1975, the NSA led by Dalla Chiesa was unexpectedly dissolved and its agents transferred to the anti-terrorist sections of Naples, Rome and Milan under the command of the carabinieri's regional directorates.[71] However, on 4 September, Carlo Picchiura, a former Pot Op activist and in charge of the Venetian column, was captured after a shooting in Ponte di Brenta. On 30 September, during another shoot-out in Altopascio, Paola Besuchio was wounded and captured. On 20 October, Giovanni Battista Miagostovich was arrested, then, on 10 November, Umberto Farioli.[72]

The death of Mara Cagol after those of MSI activists in Padua in 1974 marked a milestone in the history of the BR. The historic nucleus of the founders was eliminated and the BR, spilling blood, albeit accidentally, set off on a path of escalating violence.

5
MORETTI'S BR, 1975–1977

The death of Cagol and the arrest of Curcio – who joined Franceschini in prison – suddenly placed Moretti at the head of the BR. Under his leadership, the organisation matured and prepared itself ideologically and militarily to confront the state.

Strategic Change

Despite the blows received, the BR did not remain inactive at the end of 1975. On 21 October, the Turin column carried out an attack against the leader of the DC group in the city council of Rivoli and the Director of Personnel of Singer in Leini, who was lampooned after being forced to kneel with a placard around his neck. On the 29th, brigadists from the Milanese column entered the Confindustria Study Centre in Milan. Those present were tied up and the archives stolen. On 10 December, a Milanese brigade attacked the police station on Via Montecatini, destroying a van. The leaflet claiming responsibility accused the carabinieri of being the deadliest military arm of the counter-revolution 'that the bosses of the multinationals have unleashed against all the proletarians'.[1] The BR did not give up the factory grounds and on 10 December, in Turin, they set fire to the cars of six Fiat employees who were members of the *Confederazione Italiana Sindicati Nazionali dei Lavoratori* (Italian Confederation of National Trade Unions or CISNAL) and SIDA. On 17 December, still in Turin, Luigi Solera, a medical doctor at Fiat, was shot in the legs because he was accused of ignoring working accidents.[2]

In addition to their traditional strongholds of Milan and Turin, the BR began to operate in Genoa. The Genoese column was formed in early 1975 by Moretti. He stayed a few months before leaving the direction of the column to Micaletto. In 1977, the latter left for Turin and until 1980 the Genoese column was led by Riccardo Dura. According to Luigi Carli, magistrate in Genoa from 1979 to 1983, the column would have numbered from 60 to 80 militants.[3] Despite the presence of a few medical doctors and academics such as Enrico Fenzi, it had the distinction of being deeply working class.[4] It was distinguished above all by the strict respect for the compartmentalisation and clandestinely rules which gave it great military effectiveness and above all prevented the police from identifying its members and its leaders.[5]

The first action of the Genoese column took place on 8 October 1975 with a robbery at the San Martino hospital during the remittance of medical doctors' salaries. The police intervened but the BR managed to flee after a brief shoot-out in which one of them was slightly injured. A few days later, on 22 October, the first action was carried out against the Ansaldo company. One of its leaders, Vincenzo Casabona, was kidnapped, taken out of town, beaten and left in a landfill. This operation, despite its repercussions, did not however make it possible to recruit new members, especially among workers.[6]

The destruction of vehicles or the kidnapping of factory managers for a few hours appeared to be acts of justice, and the BR audience among the most radicalised workers was far from negligible. However, the majority of them did not express great enthusiasm. Between 1974 and 1976, the economic crisis changed the composition of the working-class world, where the figure of the precarious worker was on the verge of succeeding the factory worker who lost his central place in social struggles. The working class went on the defensive and turned away or ignored armed actions from now on, which the BR gradually understood. Years later, Curcio recalled the brigadists in the companies expressed their dissatisfaction with a situation they considered blocked and by their inability to act in the factories. He concluded that 'it was a symptom of a worrying decline of the working line that had characterised the historic first phase of the BR. The workers who were close to us now wanted to leave the factories to participate in the attack on the heart of state'.[7] The prospect of long-lasting urban guerrilla warfare was abandoned in favour of preparations for the direct confrontation with the state on the level of military might. This development caused the first split within the organisation. In Milan, Alunni, Pelli and Ronconi left the BR to found the *Formazioni Comuniste Combattenti* (Communist Combatant Formations). They refused the new strategic line which, according to them, was leading the BR down the path of political isolation.[8]

The shift of the brigadist strategy towards the confrontation against the state became more noticeable in 1976. The burning of two MSI militants' cars in Brescia on 7 and 9 January and the firing of a few shots against the garage of the chief doctor of the city's civilian hospital had little echo. This was not the case with attacks targeting police forces, in particular carabinieri. On 13 January, Quarto Oggiaro's barracks in Milan were machine-gunned, while the next day it was the turn of those of Molassana and San Teodoro,

A BR booklet, *Strategic Direction*, this is the cover of one from 1978. (Author's collection)

near Genoa.[9] Between 1 and 2 March, the BR, in coordination with the *Nuclei Armati Proletari* (Armed Proletarian Cells or NAP), hit carabinieri barracks across the country by setting fire to command vehicles of the Rho company in Milan, by shooting at Madonna di Campagna post in Turin, the Sampierdarena company barracks in Genoa, three barracks in Rome, including those of Quadraro and Garbatella, the Fuorigrotta barracks in Naples, the Campo di Marte post in Florence and the Via Guida barracks in Pisa.[10]

Actions were also taking place against commercial companies. On 2 April, in Milan, a group of five brigadists tried to steal the safe from the Magnetti Marelli factory guardhouse. Shots were exchanged and a security guard was injured in the legs. On 13 April, in Turin, the BR shot at the legs of a Fiat Mirafiori executive, accused of being in favour of dismissals.[11]

At the start of 1976, police forces continued to severely hit the BR. At the beginning of January, thanks to an informant, Angelo Basone was placed under surveillance in Milan, suspected of being a brigadist. He led the carabinieri to Nadia Mantovani and to an apartment on Via Maderno, where she lived with Curcio. The carabinieri led by Dalla Chiesa stormed the house and after a long and violent shoot-out, they captured Curcio and Mantovani.[12] On 22 March 1976, Giorgio Semeria was arrested at Milan station. After Cagol's death, the arrests of Curcio and Semeria meant the demise of the leadership of the Milan column.

Several months later, in a letter addressed to the other arrested militants Semeria denounced Moretti as a PCI spy. He said the communists were interested in maintaining some tension in Italian society, but at low intensity. Franceschini and others then wrote a report which they sent to Bonisoli and Azzolini asking them to investigate Moretti. It lasted a few months but did not discover anything suspicious.[13]

The BR's strategic evolution towards confrontation with the state was also reflected in changes in the structure of the organisation. While the CE was formed by Moretti, Azzolini, Micaletto and Bonisoli, the Factory Front was integrated into that of the Masses while the front for the fight against the counter-revolution was divided into two sectors, that of the police and that of the prisons. According to Valerio Morucci, the factories were then completely abandoned due to a deliberate choice of the organisation, but this vision was burlesque, because the BR never gave up the workers' struggles even if the actions against the executives and company directors became secondary to the benefit of politicians and state servants, a category that included journalists, local administrators, police officers and magistrates.[14]

On 17 May 1976, the first major trial against the BR began before the Turin Justice Court.[15] This was an opportunity to bring the clash between the BR and the state to the fore. The activists in prison decided to turn it into a guerrilla trial, that was to say to continue the struggle within the court to turn the accusers into the accused.[16] At the opening of the trial, they therefore refused to recognise the judges, to allow themselves to be questioned and above all they dismissed their lawyers. This attitude forced the court president, Guido Barbaro, to choose court-appointed lawyers. But the Turin lawyers refused this designation, which forced the court to appoint as BR's defender Fulvio Croce, civilian president of the Bar Association of Turin. Croce accepted the mission and delegated eight lawyers to attend the trial.[17] If the BR strategy at the Turin trial was a success, hindering the course of justice, their comrades not in jail also wanted to influence the trial.

The Death of Francesco Coco

In Genoa, on 8 June 1976, the BR waited for Francesco Coco, the prosecutor who had opposed the release of the prisoners of the *XXII Ottobre* group, at the entrance of the climb to Santa Brigida, a narrow street in the ancient city that he had to use in order to get home. The three brigadists, armed with pistols, a Skorpion submachine gun and an M12 Beretta, waited for the moment when Coco's escort was the smallest with, only two agents.[18] The prosecutor got out of his car at 1:38 p.m., Saponara, a police sergeant, followed him and together they started the climb. As they passed under an archway, they came across two men coming down the stairs. A third came out from behind the arch and all three started firing, killing Coco and the sergeant with 20 shots. Carabiniere Officer De Iana stayed in the magistrate's car to park it. He was still behind the wheel when two people approached him and, before he could make a single move, opened fire, killing him.[19]

Initially, the attack was scheduled for the 5th of the month, the first anniversary of Mara Cagol's death, but the operation was repeatedly postponed, until the tragic 8 June. The claim for this action referred to the Turin trial against the historical nucleus of the BR and demanded that the accused be given the status of political prisoners.

With the attack on Coco, the BR for the first time killed with premeditation. After the armed propaganda, the attack on the heart of the state began, raising the level of confrontation by accepting murder as an instrument of political struggle. On 9 June, the day for the pleadings of the lawyers appointed to defend the accused in Turin, Gallinari, claimed the murder of Coco on behalf of the BR. The trial was then postponed to 16 September pending the decision of the Supreme Court on a conflict of territorial jurisdiction with Milan.[20]

The strategy of attacking the heart of the state required the BR to establish a stronger foothold in the Italian capital. Moretti was sent to Rome to make contact with groups that had repeatedly solicited the BR, then he was joined by Carla Brioschi and Franco Bonisoli. Between 1976 and early 1977, they met former Pot Op militants such as Bruno Seghetti, Valerio Morucci, Adriana Faranda and Germano Maccari, former Maoists such as Francesco Piccioni, Luigi Novelli, Maurizio Iannelli, Stefano Petrella and autonomous activists.[21]

At the end of 1975, the BR rented a flat on Via Gradoli, which became the first base of the Roman column, inhabited first by Brioschi and Bonisoli, then by Morucci and Faranda, and finally by Moretti and Barbara Balzerini at the time of the Aldo Moro kidnapping. The first direction of the Roman column was formed by Morucci, Moretti, Bonisoli, Gallinari and Faranda. It was joined in 1977 by Balzerani and Seghetti. In a few months, the column had five brigades, 'Aeroporti e servizi', 'Torre Spaccata', 'Primavalle', 'Centocelle and 'Università', to which were joined two fronts, that of Logistics and that of Counter-revolution. It then had about 40 regulars, about 100 irregulars and as many sympathisers.[22]

At the end of the year, on 15 December, in Milan, brigadist Walter Alasia, 20, was killed in a shoot-out with a group of police agents who showed up at his home and arrested him.[23] Before dying, Alasia managed to open fire and kill Deputy Commissioner Vittorio Padovani and Police Marshal Sergio Bazzega. Son of a worker, Alasia, once close to the PCI and the LC, was identified thanks to the discovery of a BR base in Pavia where police discovered glasses, a doctor's prescription and Alasia's identity. In order to pay homage to him, the Milan column took the name of Walter Alasia column.[24]

Despite the death of Alasia, by the end of 1976 the BR seemed increasingly powerful. On 2 and 5 January 1977, two escapes, from

Francesco Coco, a prosecutor who opposed the release of the prisoners from the *XII Ottobre* group. (Open source)

Body of the prosecutor Francesco Coco, assassinated by the BR on 8 June 1976. (Open source)

the prisons of Treviso and Fossombrone, allowed Gallinari and Enrico Bianco to regain their freedom and resume their activities in the organisation. A week later, the BR kidnapped Piero Costa, the son of former Confindustria president Angelo Costa, who was released in April after paying a ransom of 1.5 billion lire, thanks to which the organisation could fund its activities for years to come.

Walter Alasia, a brigadist killed in a firefight with the police in Milano on 15 December 1977. (Open source)

On 13 February, the Roman column carried out its first action by wounding the director of the Ministry of Grace and Justice and delegate for the control of prisons.[25]

The 1977 Movement

1977 was a violent year in Italy. It appeared to be the height of the social conflict that arose in 1968, with the difference being that the working class, in full swing, was almost absent in 1977. For this reason, the BR remained aloof from the movement and pursued their own strategy. They rejected generalised violence in favour of targeted violence capable of lasting over time and above all of having a clear political meaning.

The movement of 1977 began with the student mobilisation in Naples and Palermo in December 1976 against the reform of the university. It then developed in the rest of the country and in February the mobilisation was general. The movement asserted itself 'autonomous' and did not define counter-projects or demands. On 18 February, in Rome, Luciano Lama, the CGIL Secretary General, was forcibly driven out from the university by thousands of autonomous young people led by Antonio Savasta and Emilia Libera who would then join the BR.[26] It was the rupture between the student movement and the workers' organisations. In the days which followed, the demonstrations multiplied against the government but also the PCI. On 11 March, in Bologna, a protester was killed by the

A demonstration in Bologna during the '1977 Movement'. (Author's collection)

An M113 armoured personnel carrier of the 37 'Ravenna' Mechanised Brigade, Folgore Division of the Italian Army, seen while deployed in Via Zamboni, in the university district of Bologna, on 11 March 1977. (Albert Grandolini collection)

Italy seemed to sink more and more into a spiral of violence between street clashes and individual attacks. Between the end of May and the beginning of July, the health manager of Seveso was injured in Desio on 19 May, on 9 June in Milan it was the turn of a foreman from Breda, and on the 20th a foreman from SIT-Siemens. On 22 June in Pistoia, the DC deputy secretary of Breda was injured as well as, on 24 June in Milan, the president of the medical association and secretary of the Order of Physicians. On 27 June, in Naples, the man in charge of relations with the personnel in Alfa Sud company was attacked. On 7 July in Padua, a journalist from *Gazzettino* was beaten. On 4 August, in Turin, Attilio Di Napoli and the Chilean refugee Aldo Marin Pinones were killed by their own explosive devices. In September, after the death of an LC activist during a demonstration outside the MSI headquarters in Rome, protests across Italy culminated in the burning of a bar frequented by right-wingers in Turin, where a student died in the fire.[30] On 18 September, *L'Unita* editor-in-chief Nino Ferrero was injured in Turin and on 20 October Rocco Sardone was killed while building a bomb in Turin.[31] 1977 was thus marked by an increase of 77.62 percent of attacks against property compared to 1976, which meant an attack every four hours during this year.[32]

police. Everywhere on 12 March, large demonstrations took place – armouries, restaurants, public places were looted by armed marches. If at first it was a student movement, it gradually went on to bring together young proletarians and those left behind by the austerity policy accepted by the PCI.[27]

On 21 April, in Rome, during a series of clashes, police agent Settimio Passamonti was shot and killed, and three other policemen were injured. Interior Minister Cossiga then banned parades in the capital.[28] On 12 May, the Radical Party organised a demonstration in Rome, while the autonomous also wanted to demonstrate to break the ban. A clash ensued in which a student, Giorgiana Massi, was killed.[29] Two days later, a demonstration against the repression turned into a confrontation again and a carabinieri non-commissioned officer was shot in the head.

If, as an organisation, the BR remained isolated from the 1977 movement, some militants, in particular those of the Roman university brigade, took part in it. The climate of violence that accompanied it could not fail to stimulate the BR's action. However, this did not mean a direct relationship between the two. For Moretti;

> this movement will remain an unknown object until the end … we have very little interacted with this movement. He was close to us by the radicality of his demands, by his nature totally foreign to institutional mechanisms and by the maturity of his practices, but he was also very distant from us by his inability and even his refusal to give himself a direction, a goal.[33]

The critique of the daily life of the 1977 movement, its festive dimension and its rejection of any authoritarian centralisation

Another M113 deployed in support of the police forces, on the streets of Bologna. (Albert Grandolini collection)

distanced it from brigadist Marxism. Nonetheless, it provided numerous recruits to the BR, notably in Rome with Libera, Seghetti and Savasta.[34] If for Gallinari 'with the young people of 1977 there were more differences than points of contact', he added: 'a large part of this Movement is knocking on our door to ask to be framed under the Red Brigades political line.'[35]

NAP and Prima Linea

It is true that the BR were not the only left-wing armed struggle organisation that existed in Italy. Several other clandestine formations developed and some ended up merging within the BR. At the end of 1974, the *Nuclei Armati Proletari* (Armed Proletarian Cells or NAP) had appeared. A meeting point between LC militants with under-proletarians and prisoners, this organisation, established above all in Lazio and Campania provinces, sought to politicise prisoners who were considered as proletarians who could be mobilised against the capitalist system. It mainly struck targets linked to the prison system and was also distinguished by the use of explosives, usually used by the extreme Right. In May 1975, the NAP kidnapped Giuseppe Di Gennaro, magistrate of the General Directorate of Prevention and Punishment Institutes and released him five days later. On 26 January 1976, they wounded a councillor of the Court of Cassation. On 14 December, during an attempted kidnapping of a magistrate, an exchange of gunfire broke out between the NAP and the police, resulting in the deaths of a police officer and an NAP activist. On 22 January 1977, the organisation enabled the escape of two activists from Pozzuoli prison. On 1 July, during a shoot-out with the police, an activist was killed and two of the January escapees were arrested again. At the end of 1977, the police force's blows nevertheless put an end to the NAP adventure, and 22 activists were sentenced to long prison terms. Those who managed to escape arrest joined the BR.[36]

At the end of 1976, a new armed struggle group appeared, *Prima Linea* (Front Line or PL), formed in Milan by former members of LC, Pot Op and young people from the autonomous movement. This group did not have an organisation as rigid as that of the BR because it wished to stay in touch with the social forces in whose name it acted. Their first action was the irruption at the Fiat executive headquarters in Turin on 30 November 1976. On 12 March 1977, PL committed its first assassination in Turin, that of the carabiniere Giuseppe Ciotta. From 1976 to 1981, the organisation claimed 101 armed actions which, according to justice, resulted in 16 victims, including magistrates or members of the police forces.

There were still many other smaller armed groups such as *Azione rivoluzionaria* (Revolutionay Action), influenced by the RAF and situationism and active in Lombardy, Piedmont, Tuscany and Liguria until 1979 when its remnants joined PL, as did some members of the *Proletari Armati per il Comunismo* (Armed Proletarians for Communism). The *Unità Comuniste Combattenti* (Communist Combat Units) existed until 1979, the *Squadre Proletarie di Combattimento per l'Esercito di Liberazione Comunista* (Proletarian Combat Teams for the Communist Liberation Army) until 1978, the *Nuclei Communisti Territoriali* (Territorial Communist Cells)

Frequently associated with *Brigate Rosse*, this photograph actually shows Giuseppe Memo, a member of the Armed Proletarians for Communism (*Proletari Armati per il Comunismo*, PAC), during a firefight with security forces in the Via De Amicis, in Milano, on 14 May 1977. (Photo by Paolo Pedrizzetti; via Albert Grandolini)

and the *Reparti Comunisti d'Attaco* (Communist Attacking Units) until 1980.

The Struggle Against the State in 1977

In this climate of diffuse violence, the BR did not remain inactive. On 11 October 1976, they injured a Fiat executive in Turin and a DC municipal councillor on the 24th. On 16 November, they shot the deputy director of *La Stampa*, Carlo Casalegno, who died on the 29th.[37] They attacked and injured an Ansaldo manager on the 30th, an Alfa Romeo manager on 8 December and one from Fiat on the 10th. The list of actions in the first half of 1977 was important even if all of them only caused injuries: on 12 February, in Rome, the Ministry of Justice director, on the 18th in Turin the Fiat Rivalta director of personnel, on 20 April, the secretary of the public prosecutor's office in Turin and municipal councillor of the DC, and two days later a Fiat Mirafiori factory foreman.[38]

This action list showed that while the BR always hit corporate executives, state officials were not forgotten as a new target emerged – journalists. According to the BR, the press became an instrument in the hands of power to manipulate information. It was the weapon of the state's psychological warfare against revolutionaries and as such became an adversary. After the attack which caused the death of Casalegno, it was the deputy director of *Secolo XIX* in Genoa, who received injuries to his legs on 1 June 1977. The next day, Indro Montanelli, director of *Giornale*, suffered the same fate, followed on 3 June in Rome by the director of the television news channel TG1.[39]

In addition to the campaign against the press, the second half of 1977 was marked by an acceleration in the number of BR actions. The Roman column wounded the dean of the economics and trade faculty of the Sapienza University of Rome on 21 June. On 11 July it was the turn of the Lazio regional secretary of the conservative organisation Communion and Liberation to be injured, while on 2 November 1977, a DC regional advisor was shot in the legs.[40] The Genoese column fired on an Ansaldo leader on 28 June, while on 11 July it hit the DC regional secretary. On 30 June, two Fiat executives were injured in Milan and Turin, while on 13 July in the Piedmont capital, a DC provincial councillor was injured. On 11 October, the head of trade union relations at Mirafiori was also injured.[41] On 23 October, in Milan, a group of BR shot a DC city councillor and the next day a Turin DC city councillor was injured. On 8 November in Milan, an Alfa Romeo manager was attacked, as was the head of the Fiat Mirafiori social analysis office on 10 November. On 17 November, the Genoese column attacked the Ansaldo Nucleare director, Carlo Castellano, a member of the PCI Ligurian regional committee.[42]

The beginning of 1978 did not mark a pause in the rhythm of the attacks which were carried out by all the columns. On 10 January in Turin, a Fiat executive was injured while in Rome two days later the director of the SIP was shot dead.[43] In Genoa, on 18 January, the higher school director and member of the DC provincial committee was injured. On 24 January in Milan, SIT-Siemens leader Nicola Toma was attacked, and then on 14 February in Rome a magistrate, Ricardo Palma, was fatally injured. Palma was part of the Commission for the Diversification of Prison Structures and Institutions with Dalla Chiesa. He had directed the restructuring of the La Marmora barracks in Turin which on 9 March hosted the resumption of the trial against the BR historic nucleus.[44]

The organisation remained committed to preventing the resumption of the Turin trial. On 28 April the lawyer and president of the Bar Association, Fulvio Croce, returned home accompanied by two secretaries. A young woman walked up to him to ask for information while a man behind him called him. He turned and the man, brigadist Micaletto, shot him with a Nagant M1995 pistol. The

Raffaele Fiore (standing), seen during his trial, with Angela Vai. (Albert Grandolini collection)

The location of *Brigate Rosse*'s assassination of the lawyer Fulvio Croce, on 28 April 1978. (Open source)

Agusta – an Italian helicopter manufacturer from Samarate – was founded in 1923 and became involved in helicopters in 1952 when it began producing Bell's designs under licence. As well as designing several machines of its own, in 1966 the company launched production of the licensed Agusta-Bell AB.205, hundreds of which were rolled out by the early 1970s. Dozens of AB.205s were acquired by the Carabinieri, who usually operated them in this simple livery, consisting of dark blue overall, and white on upper sides. Eight Carabinieri-flown AB.205s received a hoist over the right side of the cabin, but – even though this force was under the control of the armed forces until the early 2000s – they were never armed. (Artwork by Luca Canossa)

The next logical step in Agusta's operations was the acquisition of the licence for production of the highly successful Bell 206, one of the most popular helicopters around the world: this was initiated in 1967. Agusta manufactured at least three major variants: the AB.206A and AB.206B were military versions, hundreds of which were acquired by the Italian armed forces, Iran, and Sweden. AB.206C-1s were manufactured for the *Polizia di Stato* (a total of 34, starting in 1971), and for the Carabinieri (43, starting in 1974). Helicopters of both services saw intensive deployment – even if little 'direct' action – during the fight against the *Brigate Rosse*. (Artwork by Tom Cooper)

The Agusta Bell 212 was a more powerful version of the Bell 205, retaining a two-blade main rotor, but with a stretched fuselage and powered by a Pratt & Whitney Canada PT6T-3 Twin-Pac engine consisting of two coupled PT6 power turbines. Twenty-four were delivered to the 1st (Pratica di Mare), 2nd (Milano Malpensa), 3rd (Bologna), 4th (Palermo), 6th (Naples/Capodichino), and 11th (Pescara) Flights (*Reparto Volo*) of the Polizia di Stato, starting in 1976. Many were considerably modified in recent times, primarily through the addition of a FLIR-turret under the nose. (Artwork by Luca Canossa)

When 'in action', militants of the *Brigate Rosse* wore no uniforms and wore no insignia, but typical contemporary civilian clothes, nearly always topped by black balaclavas. This one is shown armed with one of a few 9mm Browning Hi-Power semi-automatic handguns: while one of the most influential pistols in the history of small arms, it remained a rare appearance in the BR's arsenal. (Artwork by Renato Dalmaso)

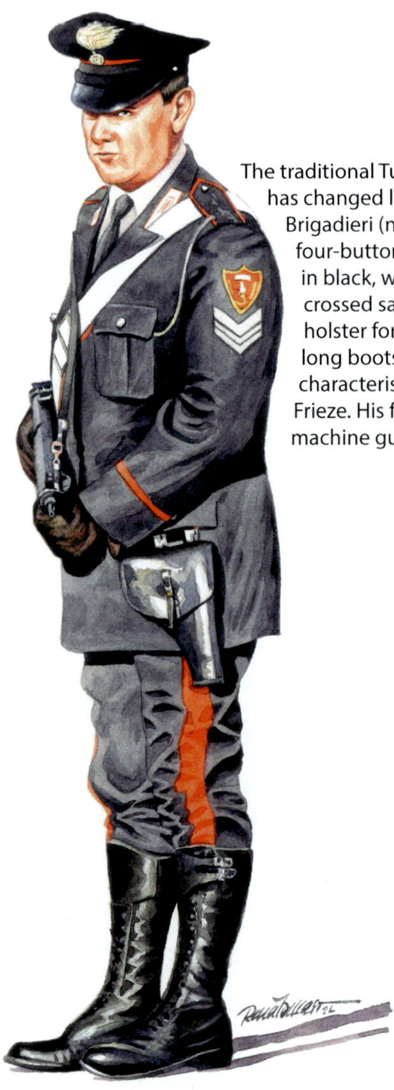

The traditional Tuscany uniform of the Italian Carabinieri has changed little since its first design in 1814. This Brigadieri (non-commissioned officer) is shown in a four-button jacket with shoulder pads and pants in black, with red accents and stripes. A white, crossed sash, black leather gloves, traditional holster for a Beretta 92 semi-automatic pistol, and long boots with laces complete his uniform. A very characteristic item was the rigid cap with a Basque Frieze. His firearm is a Beretta PM-12 series sub-machine gun. (Artwork by Renato Dalmaso)

This illustration shows an officer of either the 2nd or 3rd Celere Unit in anti-riot gear, as deployed in Bologna in 1977. Atop of his uniform, consisting of a dark blue jacket and blue-grey trousers, he is shown wearing a riot helmet with visor, crossed sashes and belt in white, with a holster for a Beretta 92, and a rubber-coated police baton. (Artwork by Renato Dalmaso)

Established in 1974, the Central Security Task Group (*Nucleo Operative Centrale die Sicurezza*, NOCS) became a tactical unit of the *Polizia di Stato*, Italy's national police, for anti-terror operations. Their attire early on was quite diverse, though usually consisting of blue overalls and blue or black ballistic vests, always topped with black baklava caps. Firearms usually included Beretta 92 pistols and Heckler & Koch MP5 submachine guns. (Artwork by Renato Dalmaso)

The Special Intervention Group (*Gruppo d'Intervento Speciale*, GIS) was established in 1978 by the Carabinieri. At that time, its operators usually wore dark blue uniforms, sometimes helmets, knee pads, elbow pads or black bulletproof wests, composed of fireproof and insulating materials. As well as the Beretta 92, the primary firearm early on was the Beretta PM-12 series submachine gun, shown here. Together with the NOCS, the GIS distinguished itself through highly excellent preparation and numerous highly efficient operations. (Artwork by Renato Dalmaso)

This infantry soldier of the Italian Army (*Esercito Italiano*) is shown as equipped while deployed on anti-riot duties in Bologna in 1977: wearing the green-overall combat uniform of the period, topped by a riot helmet with a visor, and a canvas belt carrying additional equipment, like hand-cuffs and the rubber-coated police baton. His weapon was an old-fashioned Carcano carbine, adapted to launch tear-gas grenades. (Artwork by Renato Dalmaso)

The Carabinieri, in addition to the police, acquired Agusta-Bell 206 helicopters: this one was photographed in the early 1990s. (Photo by Daniele Mattozzi and Stefano d'Amadio)

Helicopters belonging to the Italian Army were involved in some operations against the BR. Contrary to those of the police, they could – and often were – armed: this Agusta-Bell 206 was photographed in the early 1990s, with a GAU-2B mini-gun installed on the side of the rear cabin. (Photo by Daniele Mattozzi and Stefano d'Amadio)

Front view of an M113A1 armoured personnel carrier of the 37 Ravenna Mechanised Brigade of the Folgore Division, as deployed in Bologna in 1976–1977. (Photo by Marco Giuliani)

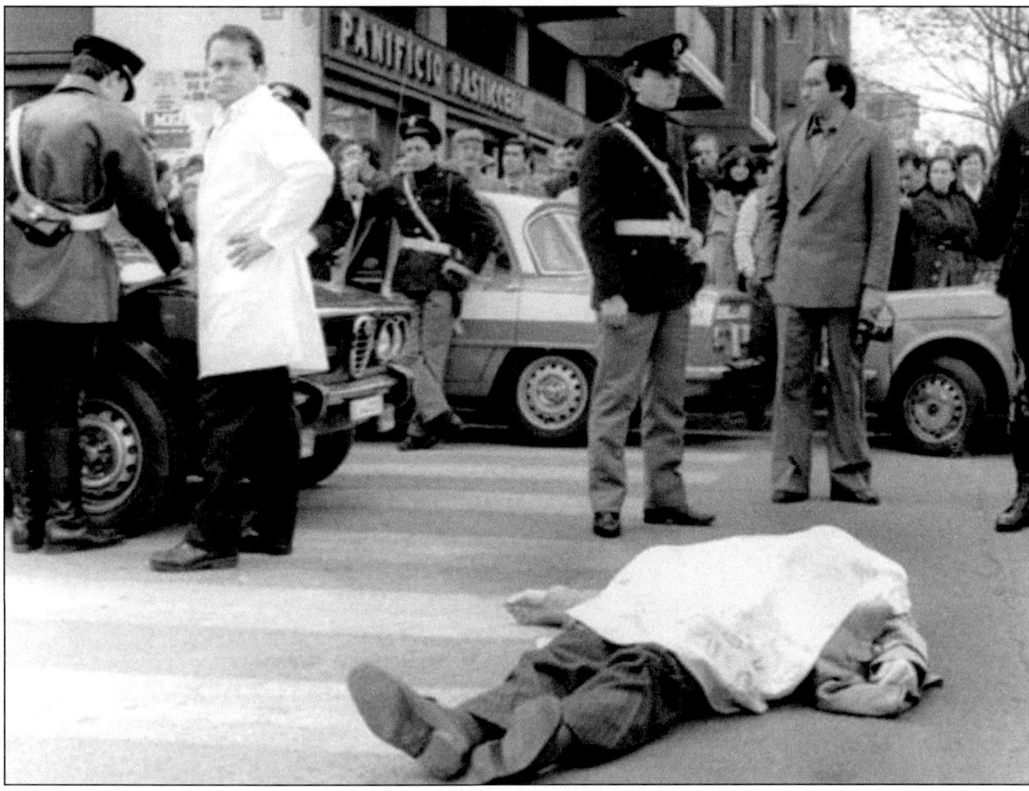

The body of Francesco di Cataldo, Deputy Commander of the San Vittore prison in Milano, assassinated by the Alasia column of the BR on 20 April 1978. (Albert Grandolini collection)

shooter and the young woman, Angela Vai, fled in a Fiat 500 driven by Raffaele Fiore.[45] This action dissuaded citizens from agreeing to serve on juries in the Turin trial for fear of reprisals. On the eve of the first hearing, on 14 June, the lawyers renounced their defence mandate. Due to the impossibility of constituting a jury, the court had to indefinitely postpone the holding of the trial.[46]

It was in this context that on 10 March, Public Security Marshal Rosario Berardi, who served in the counter-terrorism unit, was killed in Turin. On 21 June, in Genoa, the head of the city anti-terrorism unit was shot dead in his turn. In addition to these police officers, the BR hit prison officials by killing Lorenzo Crugno, an agent of La Nuove prison, in Turin on 11 April,[47] and on 20 April 1978 the deputy commander of the San Vittore prison in Milan. Despite these attacks, the BR trial resumed and ended with 29 convictions and 16 acquittals.[48]

The BR's activity since 1976, under the leadership of Moretti, was impressive in terms of number and diversity of targets and geographic extent. The fall of the historical nucleus was quickly overcome and the organisation resumed the initiative on a scale hitherto unknown. Carried away by this momentum and faced with a state that showed its weakness throughout 1977, the BR leadership began to discuss the need, in order to respond to the Turin trial, to promote a counter-trial against the DC by kidnapping a prominent politician.

Towards Operation Fritz

In the spring of 1977, the BR supervised various politicians such as Andreotti, Fanfani and Moro, without this materialising at the operational level due to numerous logistical difficulties.[49] In the autumn, Moro's surveillance resumed after Bonisoli found out that the DC president visited Santa Chiara church in Piazza dei Giuochi Delfici every morning.[50] The decision to kidnap him, despite the political and logistical difficulties of such an action, was then taken.[51] For the BR, this action had to make it possible to disarticulate the enemy forces and constituted the last period of the armed propaganda phase which had to lead to the revolutionary civil war led by the nascent fighting communist party.[52] According to Anna Laura Braghetti, the objective was:

> to open a breach in the heart of the state, a breach that would have considerably weakened the state. We do not think it would collapse as some have said, but at least we thought it would be a terrible blow that would make it tremble on its foundations, which were rather weakened at this time of intense social struggles and crises of all kinds.[53]

The BR decision was nonetheless inseparable from the Italian political situation. Since 1974, Berlinguer had declared himself available to form a government of national unity in order to put an end to the authoritarian abuses which made him fear a Greek or Chilean scenario in his country. Moro, too, was convinced of the need for the collaboration of democratic forces to stabilise Italy and put an end to terrorism and the threat of a coup. A process of convergence between the PCI and the DC called 'historic compromise' began.

The electoral campaign for the regional elections of 15 June 1975 was organised by Fanfani in the name of anti-communism after the bitter DC defeat in the 1974 referendum on divorce. The result was a victory for the Left and the PCI obtained 33.4 percent of the vote. Fanfani had to then resign from the secretariat of his party to be replaced by Benigno Zaccagnini. The latter then declared that he wanted to create the political conditions for an open confrontation with the communists, a political line supported by Moro.

Enrico Berlinguer, head of the PCI in the mid-1970s. (Open source)

Meeting between Berlinguer (left) and Moro. (Author's collection)

On the PCI side, the national elections of 25 June 1976 rewarded Berlinguer's expectations since the communists obtained the highest score in their history with 34.4 percent of the vote. Nonetheless, the DC also claimed victory as they scored higher than the PCI. The DC formed a government around Andreotti with the tacit PCI and PSI agreement who abstained in the vote of confidence to new government. The heaviest defeat was suffered by the extra-parliamentary Left which obtained only 550,000 votes which made it negligible in the context of a possible Left government.[54]

Washington was worried about the historic compromise and in September 1974, Secretary of State Kissinger asked Moro, who was visiting the United States, to end this rapprochement. He threatened: 'Either you stop it all, or you will pay dearly for it.'[55] He feared that a possible entry of the communists into the government would undermine the Atlantic Alliance.[56] Relations between Moro and Washington had been bad since in 1973 while the DC statesman, then foreign minister, refused to allow the use of NATO bases in Italy to supply US fighters to Israel at the time of the Yom Kippur War. The situation did not improve with the election of Jimmy Carter to the White House and the subsequent appointment of Cyrus Vance as Secretary of State in place of Kissinger.[57]

In 1978, to resolve a new crisis opened by the resignation of the Andreotti government, the communists demanded to participate in an emergency government. In order to unblock the situation, Moro succeeded in convincing the DC parliamentary groups to agree to the formation of a government of national solidarity led by Andreotti but supported by an enlarged majority in the PCI. 16 March was the day when Andreotti, after being sworn in before the President of the Republic, Giovanni Leone, had to appear before Parliament to ask for his confidence and receive the support of communist parliamentarians. Moro was the main architect of the historic compromise and this success placed him at the centre of the Italian political system. Many then thought he would be the natural candidate for the presidential election in December.[58]

It was in this context of agreement between the PCI and the DC that in February 1978, the BR's DS, meeting in Velletri, decided to strike at the top of the state. The Resolution it wrote asserted that Italy was the weak link in the Western imperialist chain and that the country's instability forced the government to restructure around an alliance between the DC and the PCI to ensure bourgeois domination. Faced with the historic compromise, the BR said they wanted to strike capitalism in order to 'disarticulate the forces of the enemy' of which Moro would be the most striking symbol and to 'move from the stage of armed peace to that of war'.[59]

Behind this ideological jargon, the BR leadership persuaded itself to be the last revolutionary bulwark against the PCI which supported the DC and thus showed its true 'reformist' intentions. For Moretti, the BR wanted to explode the contradiction between the base of the PCI and its leaders in order to prevent historic compromise and pushed the communist leadership to act, if not for revolution, at least for social transformation.[60] It also seems that the organisation wanted to convince the PCI militants and of the Left in general that armed struggle was the last resort to bring the revolutionary myth to life. The unfolding of Operation Fritz, the kidnapping of Moro, would prove to it that it was sorely mistaken.

6
THE MORO KIDNAPPING

The Aldo Moro kidnapping was the most spectacular operation ever carried out by the BR. It was not only through the political and media coverage it produced, but also through the operational capacities of the organisation. Long after, some still believed that it was only possible with the help of outside elements, giving rise to multiple conspiracy theories. But while the operation was a tremendous military success, it quickly turned into a political disaster for the BR.

The Via Fani Attack

On the morning of 16 March 1978, Aldo Moro prepared to experience a historic day. For the first time in over 30 years, a DC government would receive the support of PCI deputies. At around 9:00 a.m., he left his home at 79 Via Forte Trionfale in the Monte Mario district to go to Centro Studi Alcide De Gasperi, on Via della Camillucia, for a meeting with Zaccagnini, secretary of the DC. Then he had to go to the Church of Santa Chiara, in Piazza dei Giuochi Delfici, where he prayed every day, and finally to the Montecitorio Palace, seat of the Chamber of Deputies, where the investiture vote of the Andreotti government would take place.[1]

Moro joined his five bodyguards and climbed into the back of his Fiat 130. In the car was carabiniere Domenico Ricci who was the driver and, seated next to him, carabiniere Oreste Leonardi, chief of the escort. The two carabinieri knew Moro well. Ricci, 44, had been his driver since 1958 while Leonardi, 52, had been his bodyguard for about 15 years. The other three members of the escort, police officers Raffaele Iozino, Giulio Rivero and Francesco Zizzi, got into a white Alfetta following Moro's car.[2]

At 8:45 a.m., a group of nine brigadists arrived at the intersection of Via Fani and Via Stresa. Moretti stopped behind the wheel of a Fiat 128 with a diplomatic plate immediately after Via Sangemini. Alvaro Loiacono and Alessio Casimirri were in a white Fiat 128 right in front of him. A blue Fiat 128 was parked by Barbara Balzerani beyond the intersection with Via Stresa. A fourth car, a blue Fiat 132 with Seghetti on board, was on Via Stresa, parked on the left side opposite the direction of traffic, ready to reverse into the middle of the intersection. A fifth car, an empty Autobianchi A112 was parked on the right side of Via Stresa, 20 metres from the intersection with Via Fani.[3]

Moro's two cars entered Via Fani which led to Via Trionfale. At the crossroads between Via Fani and Via Stresa, up to the Olivetti bar, near the kiosk of a still closed flower shop,[4] a group of people were waiting. It was made up of Rita Algranati, carrying a bouquet of flowers in her hand, and four men dressed in Alitalia pilot uniforms, Raffaele Fiore, Franco Bonisoli, Valerio Morucci

Aldo Moro with his bodyguards. (Author's collection)

The scene of the attack on Moro's convoy in the Via Fani, on 16 March 1978. (Albert Grandolini collection)

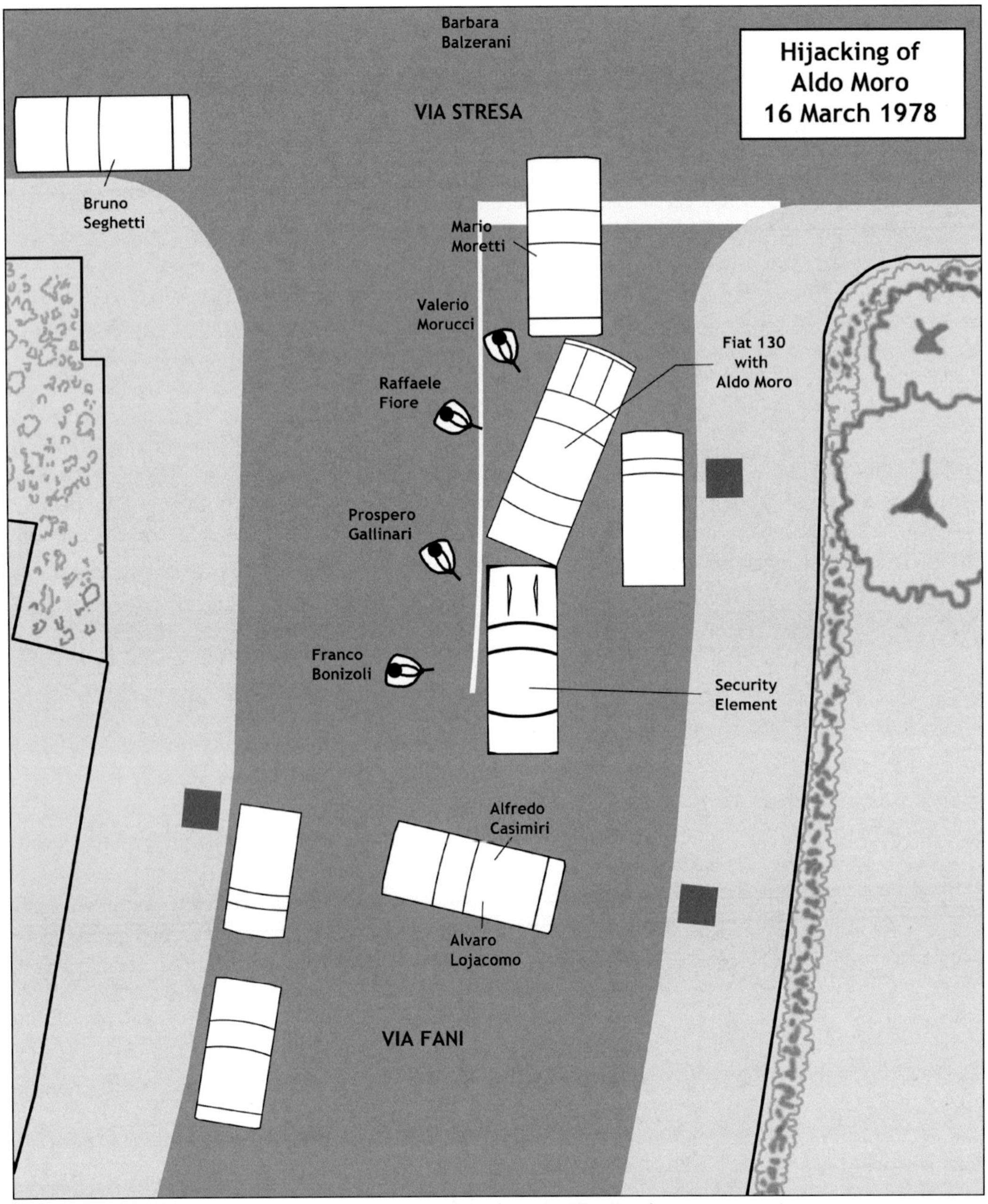

A diagram of the BR attack on Moro's convoy on 16 March 1978. (Diagram by Tom Cooper)

and Prospero Gallinari. They seemed to be waiting for the bus to Fiumicino airport.[5]

As Moro's procession appeared on Via Fani, Rita Algranati got on her Vespa and drove past Moretti's car which moved forward, turned left from Via Trionfale into Via Fani and ended up in front of Moro's escort. At the intersection of Via Fani and Stresa where there was a stop sign, Moretti's Fiat 130 came to a sudden stop, a little askew to fill the width of the lane. Behind it, Moro's Fiat 130 came to a stop as did the Alfetta.[6]

This was when the four false pilots, divided into two groups, went into action. While Bonisoli and Gallinari fired on the Alfetta, Morucci and Fiore targeted the Fiat 130. Balzerani, who was in the lower part of Via Fani, used his machine gun to block another car which was driven by an off-duty policeman.[7] In the upper part of Via Fani, it was Casimirri and Loiacono who blocked the access with their Fiat 128.

The first shots hit the driver of the Alfetta who then jerked forward, hitting Moro's Fiat. Ricci, at the wheel of the latter, started pushing Moretti's car to try to get out. In the meantime, the machine gun aimed at him jammed, as did the one that had killed Marshal Leonardi moments earlier. Ricci had time to attempt a desperate manoeuvre to get the car to safety, trying to pass to the right of Moretti's Fiat. To obstruct this attempt, the latter, instead of exiting the car as planned, stayed inside with his foot on the brake, preventing the Fiat 130 from breaking the vice it was in. Finally, Ricci was shot by a few bullets. Meanwhile, a third submachine gun fired at the Alfetta also jammed, allowing Agent Iozzino, probably already injured, to step out of the car and try to retaliate. He shot a brigadist, but he was killed by Bonisoli with his 7.65mm calibre pistol.[8]

When the shooting ceased, Moretti seized Moro and pushed him into the Fiat 132 parked at the left corner of Via Fani and Stresa and driven by Seghetti. Moro was placed at the foot of the back seats and covered with a blanket. Moretti sat down next to the driver and Fiore climbed in the back. Casimiri and Loiacono's Fiat 128 picked up Gallinari.[9] Morucci grabbed two briefcases from Moro and quickly got into the last car, a blue Fiat 128, getting into the driver's seat.

When silence fell on Via Fani, four of Moro's bodyguards were dead. The fifth, Francesco Zizzi, seriously injured, died a few hours later in hospital. Ninety-one bullet casings remained at the kidnapping scene, 49 of which were fired by an FNAB-43 that was never found. All members of the BR commando were armed. Bonisoli and Morucci each had an FNAB-43 submachine gun, Fiore an M12 submachine gun, Gallinari a TZ45 submachine gun, Moretti an MAB 38/42 submachine gun, Loaicono a .30 calibre M1 automatic rifle and Balzeani a CZ 7.65mm Skorpion, though these last three did not shoot. Each brigadist was also in possession of handguns, a Smith & Wesson 39 pistol for Gallinari, a Beretta 51 for Bonisoli, three Browning HPs for Moretti, Morucci and Fiore, who did not shoot.[10]

Morucci would later say that the operation came close to failing. All the submachine guns used jammed giving Moro's car time to free itself. It could have fled if it had not been blocked by a car on its right.[11] The negligence of the security measures around Moro nevertheless favoured the BR; DC President Moro's escort did not have armoured vehicles; the men who comprised it were ill-prepared; they always took the same routes; they did not leave sufficient distance between their vehicles; and the pistol of one of the carabiniere was placed under his seat and not within easy reach.[12]

The body of one of Moro's bodyguards seen next to the car that hit the rear of Moro's Fiat 130. (Albert Grandolini collection)

Lifeless body of Moro's driver, still in his seat after the BR's attack in the Via Fani. (Albert Grandolini collection)

The BR left the area with three cars and after a few blocks Moro was transferred to a wooden box in a Fiat 850 van driven by Moretti. Finally, the box was placed in the trunk of Bragheti's Citroen Ami 8 for the last time and taken to 8 Via Montalcini, a residential area south of Rome but not too far from the centre.[13] Meanwhile, members of the commando who came from Milan and Turin to take part in the operation took the train to the north or went to shelters in Roman bases.

During his captivity, Moro was locked in a soundproof cubicle measuring 3m by 1m, without a window and hidden behind a bookcase.[14] He had contact only with Moretti and Gallinari although among his jailers were also Braghetti and Germano Maccari.[15] Moretti, who was staying in the Via Gradoli base, was tasked with questioning him. He remained in constant contact with the CE of which he was a member with Azzolini, Micaletto and Bonisoli and which met, for security reasons, in Florence in the house of Giampaolo Barbi, member of the Tuscan Revolutionary Committee[16] or in Rapallo.[17] It seems that the BR wanted to use the prestige of their prisoner to force the state to negotiate with them and thus give them political recognition. In this scenario, Moro could have been freed and the BR's prestige increased as well as their ability to enter the political game on the Left.

Moro's Imprisonment

Shortly after the Via Fani operation, the BR claimed the action with a phone call to the Ansa news agency. At 10:00 a.m., the president of the Chamber of Deputies, Pietro Ingrao, suspended the session and announced the kidnapping of Moro. At 11:05 a.m., the main unions declared a general strike. At 12:46 p.m. the proceedings of the Chamber resumed, and confidence was given, with an overwhelming majority, to the 4th Andreotti government. During the night, the Senate also voted on confidence.[18] On 18 March, the BR released their Communication No. 1 which contained the Polaroid photo of Moro sitting under a flag with the five-pointed star and the words 'Red Brigades'.[19]

The authorities were mobilising considerable forces to find Moro. More than 20,000 men were spread across Rome and the surrounding area. They carried out 37,000 searches in the country, including 7,000 in the capital. Carabinieri set up 32 checkpoints at the entrance to Rome, and the Guardia di Finanza set up 10 checkpoints on the coastline, while two police helicopters flew over the capital.[20] Each day, 12,760 police agents were active across the country, 1,294 checkpoints were set up and 673 searches were carried out. More than 6 million people were checked, or one in eight Italians.[21]

While the BR defendants in the Turin trial claimed political responsibility for the kidnapping, the political class, notably the DC and the PCI, formed what was called the firmness front which opposed any negotiations with the BR. The PCI adopted the most uncompromising line of refusing dialogue with the kidnappers. For the communists, maintaining this position of firmness was tantamount to giving a pledge of its democratic reliability. For the DC, a negotiation with the BR would result in the exit of the PCI from the majority, thus blocking the Italian political system.[22]

On 29 March, BR's Communication No. 3 was accompanied by a letter from Moro to Interior Minister Cossiga hinting at the possibility of an exchange.[23] This was the start of a series of letters from Moro to DC leaders, to representatives of institutions and even to Pope Paul VI, in order to end the policy of firmness. The next day, the DC leadership reiterated its decision to reject all ideas of negotiations.[24] A few days later, on 2 April, a strange event occurred. Near Bologna, a group of senior officials, which included Romano Prodi, organised a spiritualist session to find out where Moro was being held. A name emerged, that of 'Gradoli'.[25]

On 6 April, as the BR delivered a letter to Moro's wife inviting her to put pressure on the firmness front, around 2,000 police agents unsuccessfully searched the village of Gradoli near Bolzena, whose name was mentioned in the Bologna spiritualism session.[26] The next day, in a public letter, Eleonora Moro announced that she was dissociating herself from the firmness line, but Zaccagnini replied that there would be no negotiations.

On 15 April 1978, the BR's Communication No. 6 declared that Moro's interrogation had ended without him revealing any secrets

Aldo Moro in a typical BR photograph of their hostages. (Open source)

or making any particular confession. Moro, found guilty of all the atrocities committed by the imperialist government against the working class, was sentenced to death.[27] The PSI leadership then decided to meet representatives of the far-left in order to get in touch with the BR.[28] The extra-parliamentary Left was indeed convinced that the Moro kidnapping was a mistake and that his death would be followed by a fierce repression against the Left.[29] The PSI sought a solution by launching the idea to release a prisoner, convinced that in this case the BR would no longer be able to kill Moro. The latter then let it be known that a political declaration by the DC on the problem of the brigadist prisoners would allow Moro to be freed.

A lot of ink would flow about 18 April. That day, following water damage in a flat, the police and carabinieri discovered the BR base on Via Gradoli in Rome.[30] The flat was empty. The same day a BR Communication No. 7 was found, announcing the execution of Moro and the abandonment of his body in lake della Duchessa.[31] This communication was actually a fake, probably prepared by Antonio Chichiarelli, a forger linked to Roman organised crime.[32] Two days later, the BR issued the actual Communication No. 7 along with a photo of Moro with a copy of the 19 April *La Repubblica* to prove their prisoner was still alive.[33]

Despite these events, the DC direction reaffirmed the firmness line while the Moro family asked them to accept the conditions of the BR. On 22 April, Pope Paul VI asked the 'men of the Red Brigades' to release Moro 'without conditions'.[34] The situation seemed blocked. To break the deadlock, the BR's Communication No. 8 on 24 April, demanded the release of 13 detainees from different armed groups including brigadists Ferrari, Franceschini, Curcio, Ognibene, Besuschio and Piancone.[35] The communication was accompanied by a letter from Moro to Zaccagnini asking him, if he was executed, for his funeral to take place without the presence of statesmen or politicians.[36] The drama of Moro's kidnapping turned into a Greek tragedy.

The BR did not want Moro dead. Faranda and Morucci were opposed, and his fate was the subject of discussions that lasted for several days. Moretti postponed the fatal outcome the longest, but it was considered inevitable by all. This was why he took on the responsibility of calling Moro's house without having received a mandate from the organisation. On the 30th, he telephoned Moro's home and affirmed that only an immediate and clear intervention by Zaccagnini could save the life of the DC president.[37]

On 2 May, the PSI leader Bettino Craxi informed Zaccagnini of the names of two brigadists who could be granted pardon for health reasons in exchange for Moro's release. The proposal was refused.[38] On the 5th, Moro wrote to his wife one last time, '... they told me they are going to kill me soon. Dear Norina, I kiss you for the last time.'[39]

The BR found themselves in a deadlock. They did not anticipate that they would face unanimous state intransigence. The gamble of splitting the PCI between its base and its leadership had failed, as shown by popular demonstrations of support for Moro and the firmness policy. They also knew that an exchange of prisoners was impossible, but they refused to give up their formal recognition by the State. Finally, they understood that there was no way to get even that. Under these conditions, according to Moretti, releasing Moro would have meant the end of the BR. The decision was then made to kill him.

On 8 May, Senate president Fanfani was tasked with delivering a pro-negotiation speech at the DC leadership meeting on 9 May. But that day, Moro was put in a crate and taken down to the garage of the residency on Via Montalcini. He was placed in the trunk of a red Renault 4. Braghetti kept watch between the elevator and the main door. The prisoner

One of countless checkpoints erected by the police during Aldo Moro's kidnapping. (Albert Grandolini collection)

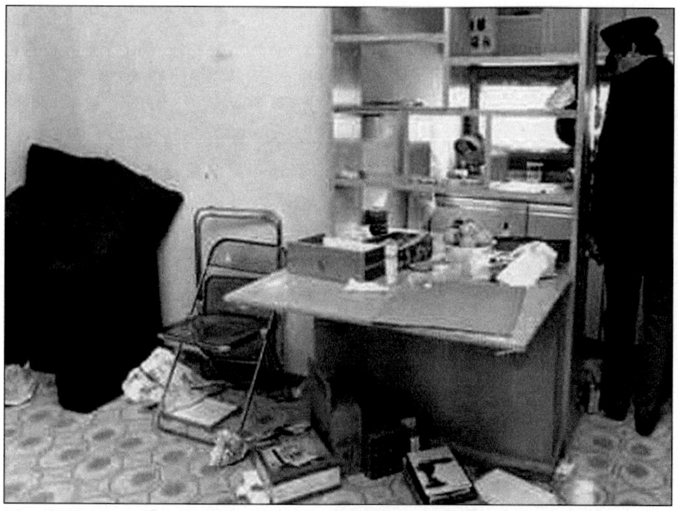

The BR base in Via Gradoli, in Rome, being examined by the police. (Author's collection)

Aldo Moro's body found inside the truck of a Renault R4, in the Via Caetani. (Albert Grandolini collection)

was covered by a blanket. Moretti shot him twice with a Walther PKK equipped with a silencer but the weapon jammed. He then took a Skorpion submachine gun and fired two more bursts. The Renault 4, carrying Moro's corpse, was driven by Moretti and Maccari along Via Caetani, halfway between the headquarters of the DC and that of the PCI. Morucci then phoned a friend of Moro's to tell him where to find the body of the DC president.[40] Moro's ordeal had come to an end. The case could begin.

The Moro Case

Moro's kidnapping and death produced many hypotheses, questions and conjectures. The number of books, newspaper articles and television programmes on these events are innumerable and each one favours a thesis to explain the drama. The first question is whether the authorities did everything to find Moro. The police forces had indeed given the impression of acting without a clear direction and in a haphazard manner. Spectacular operations such as searches did not yield any results. Police failures were numerous. Thus, on 28 March, the *Ufficio Centrale per le Investigazioni Generali e per le Operazioni Speciali* (Central Office for General Investigations and Special Operations or UCIGOS) received an anonymous phone call giving the names of five alleged brigadists. Among them there was Teodoro Spadaccini who was indeed a BR member. But it was not until 1 May that Spadaccini was spotted in the company of a printer, Enrico Triaca, an acquaintance of Moretti. A request to search his home was made only on 7 May, granted on 9 May and the search only took place on 17 May, revealing numerous documents.[41]

Anna-Laura Braghetti, who with Bruno Seghetti, took part in the assassination of Vittorio Bachelet, on 12 February 1980, as seen during her trial in 1980. (Open source)

The discovery of the Via Gradoli base summed up the weaknesses of the police forces. On 18 March, the police organised searches in the Via Cassia district, which included Via Gradoli. The occupants of flat number 11 were absent and the police did not dare to force the door.[42] Then, when Prodi, informed that a spiritualist session revealed the name Gradoli, the authorities searched the town of Gradoli in the province of Viterbo but not Via Gradoli in Rome.

These errors fuelled suspicions about the discovery of the BR flat. Was the water damage at its origin a simple domestic accident or was it intentional? In this case, was it an action of brigadists opposed to the execution of Moro who wished to put the police on the track of the latter, or even members of the Secret Service? The Via Gradoli building was in fact owned by a company which included on its directorate several members of the secret services while a carabiniere linked to these services, from the same small town as Moretti, lived on Via Gradoli and could observe the BR flat from his own. No document, no evidence, however, supports these hypotheses. What is certain is that the police services immediately disclosed to the press the news of the discovery of the flat when they could have set a trap there to arrest brigadists who could have taken them to Moro. Moretti, who was in Florence at the time, learnt the news from television and would no longer return to Via Gradoli.[43]

Many hypotheses put forward the idea that the BR were manipulated either by national forces or by foreign powers. The false Communication No. 7, written by a member of organised crime, quickly cast the Mafia shadow over the Moro case. On this point, theories advance the participation of organised crime in the Via Fani attack or its collaboration with the state in order to free Moro.[44] However, no tangible element confirms these suspicions, nor does an implication of the P2 Masonic Lodge.[45]

The role of the Italian secret services in the Moro case also appears to be non-existent. In March 1978, they were disorganised following a 1977 law abolishing the SID and replacing it with SISMI and SISDE.[46] The carabinieri organisation was also undergoing major changes following the NSA suppression. Above all, the police forces largely underestimated the BR's capacity for reorganisation after Cagol's death, which explained why the information they had at the time of Moro's kidnapping dated back mainly to 1975.[47] These different elements explained the operational failures of the police forces during the kidnapping of the DC president.

Supporters of secret service interference in Moro's kidnapping argue that certain sectors of the state were hostile to the historic compromise policy and sought to torpedo it by eliminating its main

A view of a building in the Via Gradoli where the BR held Moro. (Author's collection)

The official investigation into Moro's kidnapping and death began in the Via Fani. (Author's collection)

Judge Imposimato, investigating the Moro case, was not just looking for those responsible for the tragedy in Italy. He thus learnt that in February 1978, the French secret services were notified of the planned kidnapping of an Italian politician. For the judge, Paris played an important role in the Moro case because that was where the Hyperion Institute was located. This language school was founded in 1970 by Simioni, Mulinaris and Berio who were among the CPM founders before leaving it to found the Superclan. The Institute was becoming for many both the headquarters of European terrorism and a point of contact between the secret services of the West and the East. According to Franceschini, Hyperion would have had links with the Mossad, the CIA, the KGB and the French services.[50] The opening of an Institute agency in Rome in a building where a company was located which served as a cover for SISMI in March 1978, an agency which suddenly closed during the summer, was an element which seemed to support the idea of Hyperion's participation in the Moro kidnapping. To support this hypothesis, Franceschini did not forget to recall that Moretti was briefly part of the Superclan. Again, there is no strong evidence for Hyperion's involvement in the kidnapping of Moro, nor for that matter in the BR history after 1970.[51]

The KGB participation hypothesis also has no credibility even though the Soviet service certainly had

architect. To support their theses, they claim that the BR did not have the operational capacity to eliminate Moro's escort without the presence of a sniper among the Via Fani commando, a professional killer within organised crime or a specialist who had received military training. But then why not shoot Moro then if the purpose of the operation was to kill him? And why would this professional shooter have used a weapon dating from the Second World War and not a more modern weapon?[48] The presence of a SISMI officer near Via Fani at the time of the attack is used to confirm the thesis of secret service involvement. In fact, if this officer was present, he was not a SISMI member at this time and was in Rome on holiday.[49]

Moro monitored by a student, Sergei Sokolov.[52] The Mossad trail has also been advanced. A BR lawyer would claim that two people seen on a Honda motorbike on Via Fani were Mossad agents. Judge Imposimato found credible the intervention of the Israelis who hated Moro because of his pro-Arab policies. The CIA has also been singled out. In 2003, Franceschini even accused Moretti of having been an American agent. What is certain is that the Italian government asked for help from the CIA. The Carter administration refused the agency's involvement but agreed to send Steve Pieczenik to Rome, the deputy of the State Department's counter-terrorism cell.[53] Later, Pieczenik would present himself as the conductor of

Italian government strategy. He said he first sought to buy time to keep Moro alive in order to give the state time to take over the police, ensure the stability of the country by avoiding a government crisis, and avoid the risk of seeing PCI take power. He added that it was when Moro suggested in these letters that he could reveal state secrets that the decision was made not to deal with the BR and therefore to condemn him.[54]

We have only given here a list of the most common theories explaining the last months of Moro's life. Others accuse Andreotti of having wanted his death, some of them say that an agreement was made between the brigadists and the state. A ransom was collected by the Catholic Church but the agreement failed following a mysterious last-minute event. The BR were also accused of being in reality fascists in disguise. The thesis of a Franco-British plot to protect the interests of the two countries in the Mediterranean also exists. Most of these theories appear to be seductive intellectual constructions, often very well argued but which are sorely lacking in proof and concrete elements. They do nothing for the understanding of the Moro Case, nor for the BR's history. What is true is that the discovery of the body of the DC president plunged the BR into a period of grave crisis.

7 THE DECLINE, 1978–1981

The kidnapping and death of Moro was a trauma for the Italians and the greatest challenge to the state since 1945. The BR continued their offensive and still appeared powerful. But the authorities were determined to eliminate them and were straining all their forces to achieve their objectives. In this fight, they received the support of the majority of the population as the BR became more and more divided.

The State Strikes Back

The BR might have believed Operation Fritz was a success, especially since the actions never ceased, neither before nor during the Moro kidnapping. Throughout 1978, the presence of BR in the large factories of Turin, Milan, Genoa and Veneto was marked by various actions against hierarchies and industrial leaders. Between 10 and 31 January, a Fiat foreman in Turin, the head of the SIP public relations office in Rome and a SIT-Siemens manager in Milan were injured. The same fate befell an Italsider executive in Genoa on 4 May and a SIT-Siemens foreman in Milan on the 5th. It was the turn of a Menarini sheet metal workshop manager in Bologna on 15 May, of a Pirelli manager in Milan on 5 July, of the Small Industry Association president in Turin on 15 July, and of an Alfa Romeo manager in Milan on 29 September.[1] During this campaign, Pietro Coggiola, a Fiat workshop head, was killed with a Beretta model 81 in Turin on 29 September.[2] The BR even considered the kidnapping of Leonardo Pirelli, an action that would have been the economic counterpart to the one against Moro, but the operation was ultimately abandoned.[3]

Industrial and economic targets, however, appeared secondary in the BR's activity, who were mainly involved in the 'Spring campaign' directed against the state and its repressive forces.[4] After injuring the DC regional director of Liguria in Genoa in January, they killed, on 14 February, in Rome, the counsellor of the Court of Cassation, Riccardo Palma, seconded to the General Directorate of Prisons, then a prison guard in Turin on 11 April and another in Milan on the 20th. On 24 March, they injured the DC regional councillor Franco Picco in Torino,[5] then the former president of the Lazio regional council in Rome on 26 April and a DC section secretary in Milan on 12 May. On 19 April, the large Talamo carabinieri barracks in Rome were attacked with rudimentary bombs and a burst of submachine gun-fire. On 6 June, a prison guard in Udine was killed as was Antonio Esposito, anti-terrorist officer at the police headquarters, on 21 June, in Genoa.[6]

The attack on Esposito was carried out on the morning of 21 June at around 9:30 a.m. by a commando formed by Riccardo Dura and Francesco Lo Bianco as shooters, Adriano Duglio in protection and Luca Nicolotti as driver. Esposito got on a bus and stayed on the back platform to read a newspaper. Dura got on at the next stop while Duglio and Lo Bianco got on when the bus was already far from the centre. Duglio placed himself near the driver, his task was to force him to open the doors if necessary. Lo Bianco shot the victim with a silenced pistol. Those present started to shout and tried to exit, asking the driver to open the doors. The driver obeyed and Duglio and Lo Bianco fled while Dura fired the final shots. The three then set off in a Fiat 128 driven by Nicolotti.[7] On the same day, the public security police station in the district of San Donato in Turin was attacked.[8]

A police officer with the body of Antonio Esposito, an anti-terrorist officer of Udine, assassinated by the BR on 6 June 1978. (Open source)

Between October and December 1978, the 'Spring campaign' continued. In Rome, on 10 October, the BR fatally wounded Girolamo Tartaglione, Director General of Criminal Affairs at the Ministry of Justice.[9] On 15 December in Turin, Salvatore Lanza and Salvatore Porceddu, police officers assigned to the surveillance of Nuove prison, were killed.[10] A few days later, on the 21st, two policemen assigned to the escort of deputy Galloni were injured in Rome.[11]

The feeling of power that these many actions could inspire, besides the Moro kidnapping, was nevertheless fragile. The state was mobilised by passing special laws that increased the police powers, authorising a number of exceptions to common law, in particular as regards home searches, identity checks, the length of police custody and preventive detention. At the judicial level, the rights of the defence were reduced, and the penalties severely increased for crimes linked to terrorism.

The BR also had to face a powerful security apparatus: 80,000 carabinieri and 100,000 police officers who had already shown their efficiency in 1972 and 1974. On the side of the police, Gaspare de Francisci took over the leadership of UCIGOS in 1978, which was divided into four divisions, a general division which dealt with the international links of armed groups, a 'red terrorism' division and a 'black terrorism' division, an operational division and a specialised intervention nucleus the *Nucleo Operativo Centrale di Sicurezza* (Central Security Task Group or NOCS).[12]

Following Moro's kidnapping, Interior Minister Cossiga resigned. He was replaced by Virginio Rognoni who, on 20 August 1978, called on Dalla Chiesa to lead a reconstituted anti-terrorist group. The general obtained carte blanche to conduct his investigations in full independence, without informing the prefectures, and he was answerable for his work only to the Interior Minister. This group, made up of 180 carabinieri and 50 police officers, was divided into three geographical areas, North, Centre and South.[13] The coordinators were Nicolo Bozzo, Lieutenant-Colonel Giovani Marocco and Major Giosuè Candida. In the north, four special sections operated in Turin, Genoa, Milan and Padua under the command of captains Gian Paolo Sechi, Michele Riccio, Umberto Bonaventura and Gian Paolo Ganzer.[14] Dalla Chiesa quickly achieved success. The police had already identified the printing press of the Roman column, on Via Pio Foà, even though they only broke into it on 17 May, arresting Enrico Triaca, Gianni Lugnini, Teodoro Spadaccini, Gabriella Mariani, Rino Proietti, and Antonio Marini, and grabbing all the material.[15]

At the end of July, one of the four members of the CE, Azzolini, left a bag on a bus in Florence. The bag, in which was a rifle, was handed over to the carabinieri, who also found inside numerous documents and a bunch of keys. The investigation quickly led to Azzolini who was placed under surveillance. Keys found in his bag allowed carabinieri in Milan to open the door to an apartment at 8 Via Monte Nevoso.[16]

Azzolini, despite the loss of his bag, did not evacuate the base, nor two other bases which were also in Milan. Above all, he did not warn anyone of the risk that loomed. Thanks to a series of police activities, carabinieri managed to discover the other two bases, on Via Pallanzana and Via Melzo. On 1 October 1978, under the leadership of captains Arlati and Bonaventura, they took action and took over the Milan bases where they arrested many brigadists including Antonio Savino, Biancamelia and Paolo Sivieri, Maria Russo, Domenico Gioia and Flavio Amico.[17]

The base of Via Monte Nevoso was of great importance to the BR. It welcomed Nadia Mantovani and Bonisoli who studied there the questioning of Moro to prepare the final document on the 'Spring campaign'. The flat was full of documents including the entire BR archives since 1970 and copies of many letters and texts written by Moro during his imprisonment.[18] Given the political value of these documents, the BR built a hiding place in the base in which they placed money and weapons, as well as photocopies of the original documents written by Moro. In 1978, this hiding place was not found by the carabinieri. This error seemed to be the result of the tensions that existed between the Dalla Chiesa nucleus and the Milan carabinieri command.[19]

The blow dealt by the fall of the Via Monte Nevoso base was severe. Moretti would say: 'In October 78, two members of the Executive, Azzolini and Bonisoli and all the leadership of the column were arrested. Not a single irregular remains and the city's network is paralysed. The Milan column is in ruins.'[20]

The Death of Guido Rossa

The fall of the Monte Nevoso base marked the start of the BR crisis. Moro's kidnapping, spectacular as it was, resulted in a dead end. It had not opened up political prospects, and the state firmness, which had done nothing to save Moro, left the BR only the path of flight forward in a dead-end armed struggle. This lack of prospects was compounded by the murder of communist activist Guido Rossa. The BR then lost the residual support of the social forces they wanted to conquer.

In 1978, the Genoese column decided to establish itself in the major industrial centres and certain activists began to distribute propaganda material there. They mainly focused their efforts on the Italsider site where they were absent. Francesco Berardi, a 50-year-old worker from Puglia, who entered the factory in 1956, worked there. In 1977, he contacted the BR and offered to distribute propaganda material in his factory. He thus became an irregular in the organisation.[21] But Moro's kidnapping resulted in mobilising the unions against the BR. This struggle began a few years earlier, under the PCI leadership, but without achieving great results. Thus,

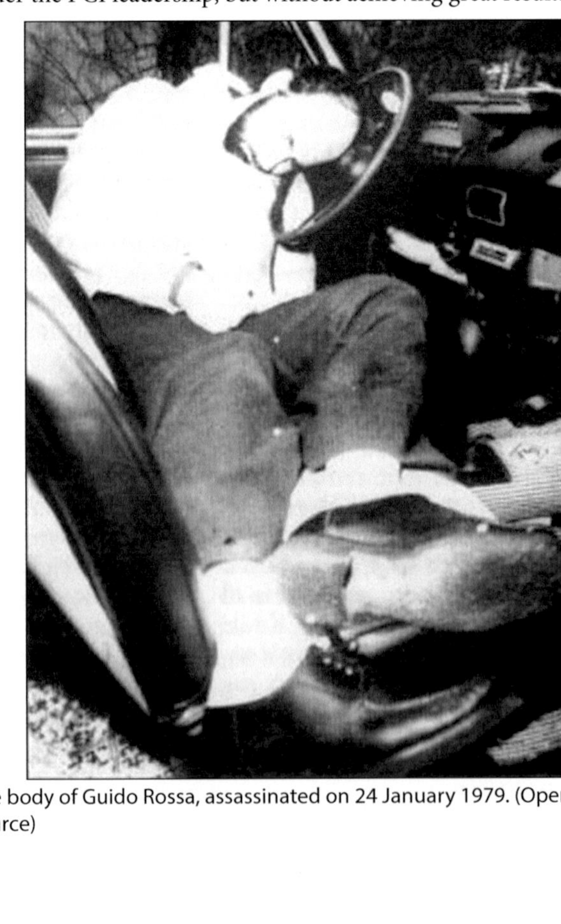

The body of Guido Rossa, assassinated on 24 January 1979. (Open source)

in 1977, the PCI Torino federation had already published 100,000 questionnaires intended to mobilise the workers against the BR. The fifth question asked: 'Do you have concrete facts to report that can help the judiciary and the police to identify those who commit attacks, crimes, assaults?' The operation was a failure. Of the 12,676 completed questionnaires, there were only 35 responses to the fifth question.[22]

The popular mobilisation to support the firmness policy during the Moro kidnapping showed a change in attitude of the workers that the unions wanted to use to incite them to denounce their colleagues involved in subversive activities. Communist trade unionists were particularly active against the BR. Their work was coordinated by the PCI leadership, which maintained relations with the Dalla Chiesa nucleus and the Interior Ministry through Ugo Peccioli.

In Italsider, Guido Rossa, PCI member and union representative, was active in the fight against the BR. On 25 October 1978, he surprised Berardi hiding leaflets under his jacket and whom he already suspected to be close to the BR. He denounced him to the carabinieri. Berardi was arrested and confessed to his propaganda activities. His trial took place at the end of the month and he was convicted of participating in an armed gang. Rossa's name was released to the media during the trial.[23]

For the BR, Rossa's gesture was a class betrayal. After a long discussion, the CE, composed of Fiore, Micaletto, Gallinari and Moretti, accepted the proposal of the Genoese column to injure the union leader in order to punish him.[24] The commando that had to strike Rossa was made up of Guagliardo, Dura and Carpi. The first was to shoot, the second cover him and the third intervene to ensure their escape. On the morning of 24 January 1979, Guagliardo and Dura hid in a van near the car park where the trade unionist parked his car. Carpi waited in a Fiat 128. As soon as Rossa appeared at 6:40 a.m., Guagliardo got out of the van, making a noise. Rossa defended himself and tried to protect his chest with his arms, but Guagliardo managed to shoot him four times in the legs before pulling away. At this point, Dura, providing cover, who must have thought that Guagliardo had missed his mark, approached Rossa's car and killed him with two shots. As soon as the news of Rossa's murder spread, the Italian Left was outraged.[25]

The Genoese workers mobilised and launched a strike lasting a few hours. The authorities decided to organise a state funeral that brought together a huge crowd of communist activists and workers from many parts of Italy.[26] The BR immediately realised the gravity of the gesture and the anger it aroused among the working class. They were initially reluctant to claim responsibility for the attack, which they did not do until the evening of 25 January. The Genoese column was criticised by the CE and the expulsion of Dura was also considered.[27] However, there was a break between the BR and the working class.

The Attack on Piazza Nicosia

Rossa's death was not the only action of the Genoese column, which was particularly active in 1979. On 29 May, it injured a DC regional councillor and on 31 May the Professor of Constitutional Law, Fausto Cuocolo, head of the DC group in the Liguria Regional Council and Dean of the Faculty of Political Science. The BR entered his classroom, pushed the professor against the wall, and shot him in the legs. At the end of the year, on 21 December 1979, in Sampierdarena, the BR killed two carabinieri, Mario Tosa and Vittorio Battaglini.[28]

The situation in Genoa contrasted with that of Milan where the organisation was decapitated by the carabinieri operation against the Monte Nevoso base or that of Rome which was hit by an internal crisis with the departure of Morucci and Faranda who left the BR in February 1979.[29] The organisation offered them a temporary base in Moiano, in the province of Perugia, with money, a gun and documents to leave the country. But Morucci and Faranda preferred to return to Rome where, on 24 March, they settled in the home of Giuliana Conforto. According to an unconfirmed hypothesis, Guido Conforto, Giuliana's father, a former Soviet intelligence agent, informed the police of their presence at his daughter's home. They were arrested on 29 May and among the weapons in their possession

A demonstration in Genoa in reaction to the murder of Rossa. (Author's collection)

The scene of the BR attack on Piazza Nicosia, on 3 May 1979, with the bodies of two killed police officers, and another badly injured, ambushed by Piccioni's group. (Albert Grandolini collection)

Police officers in civilian cothing in front of the DC headquarters at Piazza Nicosia. (Albert Grandolini collection)

Valerio Morucci was considered an expert in weapons and military organisation, and was appointed the leader of BR's column in Rome. Following his arrest and trial, he disassociated from the *Brigate Rosse* and was paroled. (Open source)

was the Skorpion machine gun with which Moro was killed.[30]

Despite the departure of Morucci and Faranda, the Roman column was still strong and capable of carrying out important actions. It decided to intervene in the electoral campaign of 1979 by attacking the Roman provincial seat of the DC, Piazza Nicosia, located in the centre of the city a few hundred metres from the Palazzo Chigi and the Parliament. The difficulties of the operation, which consisted of stealing documents and depositing small explosive charges, were numerous.[31] The aim was to coordinate the movements of 15 brigadists, including nine in the front line. The action had to take place in an unfavourable environment, the escape routes were narrow and limited by the Tiber. Proximity to state leadership centres fuelled a constant flow of police convoys and armed escorts. The location of the target in the heart of the city resulted in the presence of a large population on the streets. Finally, the DC headquarters was monitored by police officers and guards.

The preparatory meetings of the 12 men and three women who made up the commando took place in small groups. They were divided into three groups of five activists each coordinated by Gallinari, Seghetti and Piccioni. The first two had to occupy the first and second floors of the DC building while the third was responsible for ensuring the protection of the operation outside.[32]

On 3 May 1979, the inaugural day of the election campaign, the commando attacked in broad daylight. The raid began at 9:45 a.m. when the first cell, led by Seghetti, managed to break into the building after having immobilised the guards, while the second cell, led by Gallinari, watched the entrance and the third, commanded by Piccioni, remained in the street to face the possible arrival of the police. Inside the building, the brigadists handcuffed the guards and seven DC officials, stole a large quantity of documents, inscribed the slogan 'Transforming electoral fraud into class struggle' on the walls, and placed five bombs on the upper floor. Hostages were given 10 seconds to evacuate the building before the explosion.

While the commando pulled out, a DIGOS car arrived to verify a call for help made by a passer-by. The cover group and the brigadists coming out of the building opened fire. The three policemen did not even have time to get out when they were hit by several bursts fired by a Kalashnikov and an M12. The police agents fought back, but they were hit and only the youngest of the three miraculously survived. A few moments later, explosions devastated a wing of

The body of one of three police officers killed by the BR during the Piazza Nicosia attack on 3 May 1979. (Albert Grandolini collection)

the building, the brigadist commando then disappeared into the traffic.[33]

On 13 July, the Roman column swung into action again, killing carabiniere Colonel Antonio Varisco, commander of the Rome Tribunal's escort service, after a car chase. This murder marked the resumption of the campaign against special prisons.[34]

Prisoners Against the CE

The release of detained activists or the improvement of their living conditions was always one of the objectives of the BR. Since Curcio's escape in 1975, the Italian State had built special prisons with reinforced security and harsh conditions of detention. The Asinara prison, located on a small islet in Sardinia, was the symbol of these special prisons. This was where most of those convicted during the Turin trial were held, who formed a prison brigade also known as the 'kampo brigade'. In the spring of 1979, they let the organisation know that they had prepared an escape that involved 53 inmates, not all of them BR members. The CE then instructed the Roman column to prepare an operational plan and to contact Barbagia Rossa, a Sardinian armed group close to the BR, for its realisation.[35]

The BR began by establishing a base in an uninhabited hut village, Argentiera. The plan drawn up by the prisoners called for the inmates to occupy a section of the prison from which they could exit outside and reach the mainland by canoe. Their exfiltration from Sardinia required a large number of cars to move them on the island, the presence of protection groups capable of stopping the Asinara carabinieri and police agents alerted after an escape, a series of shelters to hide escapees, and offshore boats for transport to the

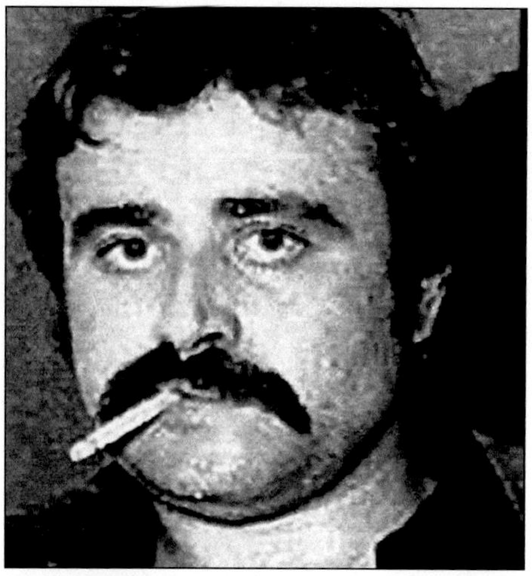
Prospero Gallinari, who survived a firefight with the police and a head wound, on 8 August 1979. (Open source)

mainland. This logistical mobilisation was, according to Moretti and Gallinari, the main reason for the refusal of the CE to implement the operation.[36] It required the engagement of all the operational forces of the organisation, with the very high risk that they would disappear forever in the event of failure. In addition, the supply of firearms to the BR was low. They then only had one Kalashnikov, the one used in Piazza Nicosia, which came from the Red Army Faction and was used during the kidnapping of the German industrialist leader Hans Martin Schleyer.[37] On 8 August, the CE, which met in Porto Torres, decided that the organisation was unable to get involved in an overly complex escape plan and postponed it until the following summer.[38]

To secure funding for the organisation as Costa's ransom money ran out, the CE charged the Roman column with conducting a suitable theft. An objective was found but, as Gallinari changed the licence plate of a stolen car in the street, he and his two comrades were noticed by a police patrol. A shoot-out began. Gallinari was badly hit in the head and arrested with Mara Nanni.[39] He was miraculously saved by the doctors, but the police found a map of Asinara island on him and clear references to the escape plan which was thus discovered.[40]

Asinara prison was searched. The guards discovered bladed weapons, but not the previously hidden plastic explosive. BR prisoners were placed in total isolation with no cell-to-cell communication. They then decided to turn the escape plan into a riot and, on 2 October, they went into action. The element of surprise did not come into play and the inmates barricaded themselves in a section of the prison. They repelled the carabinieri attacks and thus resisted for a whole night until the final assault. A week later, many of them were transferred to other prisons as Asinara prison was renovated and strengthened.[41]

The CE's refusal to carry out the plan to release the prisoners from Asinara drove a wedge between them and the organisation's free leaders. The prisoners were very hostile towards Moretti, whom they blamed for the BR's failures and the political stalemate in which the organisation found itself. As Fenzi remarked, 'they hated Moretti'.[42] Members of the historic nucleus, locked in Palmi Prison, set off down a path that took them far from the Moretti positions. Taking up Morucci and Faranda's arguments, they blamed the leadership for ignoring the potential of the 1977 movement and for distancing itself from the needs of the masses.[43] They wrote in 1979 the '*Documentone*', later published under the title *L'ape e il comunista*, a long document of over 100 pages in which they called for a discussion between all the columns concerning the strategic line to be followed. According to them, Italy was on the brink of civil

Valerio Morucci and Adriana Faranda, both of whom left the BR in 1979. (Open source)

war and Moretti's line was too bureaucratic, political, and military. They called for more attacks to trigger the outbreak of the looming civil war.[44]

Moretti and the CE refused to discuss the '*Documentone*', the analyses of which they considered to be incorrect. The response they sent to the prisoners was considered by Fenzi to be insulting.[45] The prisoners then asked for the resignation of the CE and in December 1979 the DS, convened in Genoa, a meeting at Via Fracchia. The columns of Genoa, Milan, Turin, Veneto, Rome, Naples represented respectively by Dura, Guagliardo and Nadia Ponti, Seghetti, Savasta, Nicolotti, and Renato Areni participated. The CE resigned but as it was not replaced it was again confirmed in its functions while the prisoners' theses were rejected.[46] In order to avoid a break with the prisons, the CE decided to appoint three activists, responsible for strengthening ties with the prisoners, who would form the embryo of the future Prison Front.[47]

The Via Fracchia Massacre

On the military level, in 1979 the BR continued to strike. They killed a police officer in Rome on 9 November, two carabinieri in Genoa on 21 November, a police officer in Rome on 27 November and a DIGOS marshal in Rome on 7 December.[48] They injured a policeman in Turin on 18 September, the trade union relations office head at Fiat Mirafiori in Turin on 4 October, a policeman in Rome on 31 October, and a Fiat department head in Turin on 14 December.[49]

The state reacted with Decree-Law 625 of 15 December 1979 which increased by half the sentence for crimes committed for the purposes of terrorism and extended the concept of subversive association. Subsequent articles empowered the police to arrest any person suspected and authorised them, depending on the circumstances of time and place, to carry out searches and judicial arrests for a maximum period of 48 hours.[50]

At the end of 1979, the columns of Turin and Milan suffered the most from police actions. Nevertheless, the new decade began with the development of various armed actions against state and political personnel. The campaign against police forces was the most important. On 8 January in Porta Ticinese, Milan, DIGOS agents Rocco Santoro, Antonio Cestari and Michele Tatulli were killed, a 'signal for Dalla Chiesa', according to the claim.[51] On 25 January 1980, carabinieri Colonel Emanuele Tuttobene and his driver Antonino Casu were killed in Genoa while Colonel Raimundo was wounded.[52]

On 28 January, the Venetian column attacked the petrochemical sector of Marghera by killing its deputy director, then in the autumn the former director of the same factory, Luciano Strizzoli, was pilloried. On 29 February 1980, the MGN factory personnel director was shot in the knee.[53]

These actions were nevertheless overshadowed by the murder of Professor Vittorio Bachelet, vice-president of the Supreme Judicial Council. The action, directed by Braghetti and Seghetti, took place on 12 February inside the Sapienza University of Rome following an academic conference.[54] The death of this great and deeply Catholic jurist aroused the general indignation of the population. On 18 March, the Roman column took action again, killing Girolamo Minervini, counsellor at the Court of Cassation and head of the secretary of the Institutes of Prevention and Repression.[55]

Meanwhile, the fate of the BR was playing out in the north of the country. The police conducted a major anti-terrorist operation in this region which led to the arrest in Turin on 19 February 1980 of two BR leaders, Patrizio Peci and Rocco Micaletto. Peci, after a few days, decided to collaborate with the carabinieri and provided information to Dalla Chiesa.[56]

Thanks to Peci's confession, on 28 March 1980, carabinieri surrounded the Via Fracchia in Genoa, where there was a base which housed Dura, Piero Panciarelli, Lorenzo Betassa and Annamaria Ludmann, owner of the apartment. Panciarelli and Betassa came from Turin, where they had to flee to avoid arrest. The flat had many features that made it a safe base. It was located in the basement with a backyard that allowed an emergency exit, as well as windows to the rear while thick curtains behind the glass of the front door hid the home's interior. Its location was perfect. The centre could be reached quickly but it was also located in a secluded and absolutely anonymous area, which allowed a quick escape to the mountains. There were no shops or public places nearby, making the presence of anyone outside the neighbourhood visible. The apartment also

Brigadists killed during the assault on the BR base in the Via Fracchia. (Open source)

had the advantage of legally belonging to the Ludmann family and since 1977 it had been occupied by Annamaria Ludmann who turned it into a BR base. The latter did not appear to be a member of the organisation, however, but a sympathiser whose only activity was to provide this shelter.

The scene in the Via Montenovoso in Milano, after the local BR base was discovered by the police on 1 October 1978. (Author's collection)

Carabinieri from Dalla Chiesa's Special Unit burst into the base after 4:00 a.m. A shoot-out broke out and Betassa fired a shot and the carabinieri returned fire killing the four brigadists.[57] Marshal Rinaldo Benà was injured in the eye; by Betassa according to the carabinieri; by friendly fire according to other reconstructions.[58] In retaliation after the Via Fracchia operation, on 1 April 1980, the BR burst into a Milanese DC section during a meeting with the deputy Nadir Tedeschi and shot four people in the legs.[59]

The Via Fracchia massacre was a violent blow struck against the Genoese column. For the first time, brigadists were killed and important equipment seized. But beyond that, it signalled that the State was ready to raise the level of confrontation in its fight against the organisation. Above all, Peci who knew a lot, had spoken to the carabinieri, which was also a novelty. He denounced the lawyer Edoardo Arnaldi of Genoa, long-time brigadist and seriously ill, who preferred to commit suicide when his home was searched on 19 April 1980.[60] Peci's information undermined the Genoese column but it was the Turin column that suffered the heaviest losses, not only because Betassa and Panciarelli were killed at Via Fracchia, but also because Peci revealed everything he knew about the BR of the Piedmontese capital, where he was the main leader. If the organisation doubted for a moment that Peci had become a carabinieri informant, the Roman newspaper *Il Messaggero* published part of the interrogation minutes in early May 1980 and thus uncovered the truth.[61]

The Neapolitan Column

In reaction to the attack on Via Fracchia, the BR resumed the offensive. On 7 May, the director of the regional labour office was injured in Rome, then on 12 May, Alfredo Albanese, director of DIGOS in Mestre, was killed. As he left his house in his car, another car driven by Marco Fasoli blocked him. The latter and Marino Bono shot him while Michele Galati and Nadia Ponti covered them. Albanese tried to defend himself by opening fire, but it was in vain.[62]

Nevertheless, after the summer, the police still continued to strike the Genoese column: on 18 September, on Via Peschiera in Genoa, two brigadists were arrested near the home of the mayor Fulvio Cerofolini while a third, Leonardo Bertulazzi, succeeded in escape. On 25 September, a BR warehouse was discovered on Via Montallegro, on 4 October a new base on Via Palestro fell, and on 10 October the house of 73-year-old Caterina Picasso was discovered. The police found many weapons there. In the space of about a month, seven bases fell and dozens of weapons were seized by the police along with files. On 28 October, DIGOS arrested 11 more brigadists, then 10 more between November and January 1981. The Genoese column, until then considered the least vulnerable, was now in agony.[63]

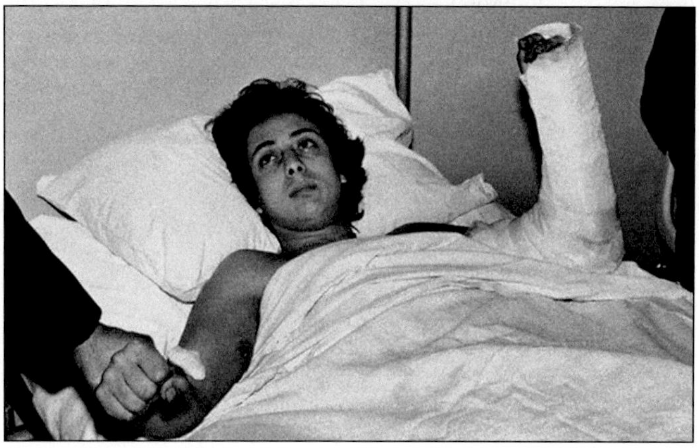

Bruno Seghetti in hospital following his arrest in May 1980. (Albert Grandolini collection)

While the Genoese BR were hard hit, a new column was created in the south of the country which played a decisive role in the early 1980s. Naples and its region presented a very different social and economic structure from that of the north, where the BR appeared and grew. The new column of BR, which was formed during 1979 in Naples, included these actions in the strategy defined by the CE. It struck the state from its first action. On 19 May, at around 9:30 a.m., a Fiat 131, with Ciro Esposito as driver and passenger Pino Amato, DC regional councillor for Campania, was blocked by a Fiat 500 driven by a woman who positioned her car in such a way as to prevent it from moving forward. From this car a commando of three men emerged who shot Amato and killed him. The driver nevertheless managed to get out of the car and shot the brigadists, who retaliated. Esposito's unexpected reaction disoriented the brigadists who, having arrived in Piazza Martiri, split up only to find themselves in a Skoda which was immediately intercepted by the police. They managed to escape, but shortly after, the police forces arrested the members of the commando, Bruno Seghetti, Maria Teresa Romeo, Salvatore Colonna and Luca Nicolotti, which represented a defeat for the column.[64]

The earthquake of 23 August 1980 which devastated Campania and destroyed part of the city of Naples marked a turning point for the Neapolitan column. The unemployed, marginalised and displaced people dominated the city, and the BR could not ignore them. They then turned to the immediate needs of this population rather than against the state and thus deviated from the strategy defined by the CE.

The Road to Splitting

The first fracture within the BR, however, was not born in the south but in their historic cradle, Milan. The Walter Alasia column was moving further and further away from the positions of the CE, which it accused of abandoning factory grounds. Moretti tried all means to maintain unity through a series of meetings with representatives of the column, but to no avail. The decisive meeting took place in the spring of 1980 on the Lazio coast, in Tor San Lorenzo, where, besides Moretti, Ponti, Balzerani, Savasta, Fenzi, Iannelli and Guagliardo, the representatives of the column, Nicola De Maria, Auroro Betti and Vittorio Alfieri were also present. The latter wanted the BR to retain their worker character and they demanded the resignation of the CE.[65] The point of view of the Milanese was close to that of the 'historical' militants detained in Palmi even if the latter wished the retention of the unity of the BR.[66]

Despite efforts to keep the organisation united, the Alasia column no longer recognised the BR's strategic line. This was a column where many of the activists were legal and worked in factories, especially at Alfa Romeo. They attached great importance to the links between the BR and the workers, especially since on 11 September 1980, Fiat announced the dismissal of nearly 15,000 workers, which led to a general strike. If the Fiat management backed off by suspending layoffs, many workers wanted to return to work and opposed the picket lines. Above all, 40,000 white-collar workers were demonstrating for the first time in the streets of Turin against the strike. The protest turned into a defeat for the Italian proletariat, which would no longer be able to oppose deindustrialisation and globalisation.[67]

A final attempt was made to keep the Alasia column in the organisation. The mission was entrusted to Fenzi and Guagliardo.[68] But on 12 November the Milanese column killed Renato Briano, director of Magneti Marelli, without the action having been approved by the CE. A few days later, on 28 November, it assassinated the Falck Unione steelworks' technical director, Manfredo Mazzanti.[69] The CE had no choice but to expel the Alasia column, which from that moment became an independent organisation.[70]

The publication, in December 1980, of the long essay written by the BRs in prison, *L'ape e il comunista*, contributed to deepening the dissent within the organisation, which was heading for a new split. The prisoners, unlike the leadership, wanted the BR to turn to the marginalised proletariat and the underclass. Their theses found an echo in the Neapolitan column directed by Giovanni Senzani. The latter, unlike the majority of brigadists, did not come from the working-class world. He was a literature graduate who specialised in sociology before becoming a criminologist. These divisions did not prevent the BR from once again demonstrating their operational capability.

The D'Urso Kidnapping

On 12 December 1980, in Rome, brigadists waited for Giovanni D'Urso, director of the Ministry of Justice General Directorate of Institutions for Prevention and Repression, in a street where he parked his car. To the right of the street was a van with Ennio Di Rocco behind the wheel and Senzani seated beside him, while in the back were Moretti, 'Rolando' and 'Daniele'. Further on, at the left side of the road, was a car with Stefano Petrella and another brigadist inside in charge of covering the first group. When D'Urso parked his car and began walking towards his home, Moretti, Rolando and Daniele got out of the van and grabbed him, putting him into the vehicle where he was locked in a wooden crate. He was then brought to Via della Stazione in Tor Sapienza on the outskirts of the capital.[71]

In the D'Urso kidnapping, the BR did not ask for the opening of negotiations with the state and involved the Palmi prisoners' committee in the conduct of the operation since the latter aimed to improve living conditions and the closure of Asinara prison. This action also aimed, in Moretti's mind, at reconciliation with the BR's prisoners and the Alasia column.[72]

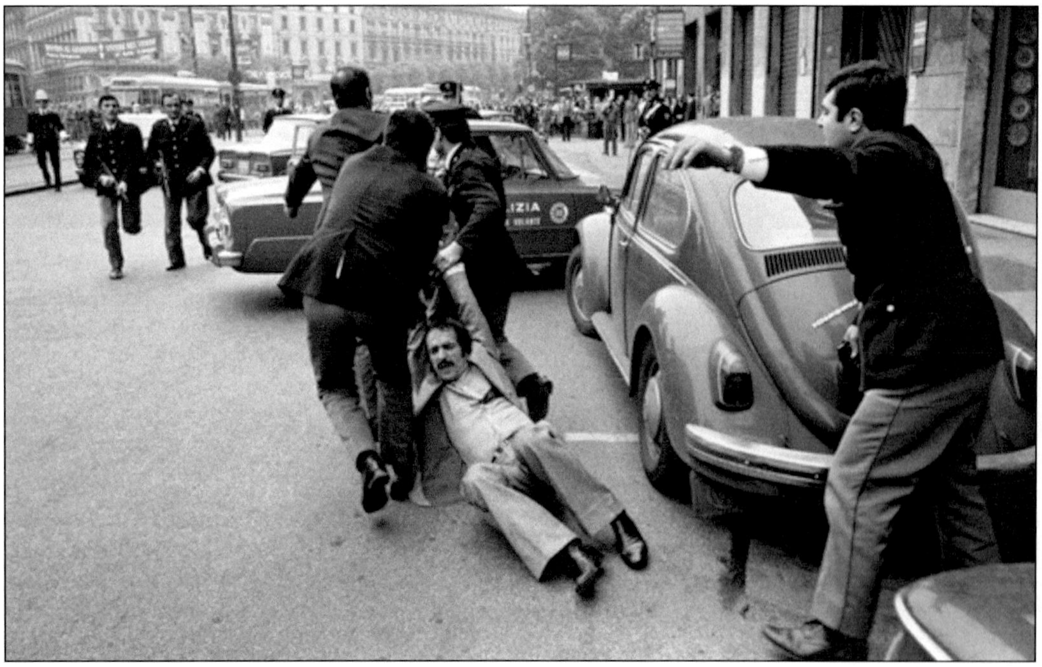
The arrest of Moretti in Milano on 4 April 1981. (Albert Grandolini collection)

Political forces and public opinion immediately took sides with a firmness policy, as was the case with the Moro kidnapping. The government followed this position as, on 21 December, the BR suffered another setback with the arrest in Turin of Guagliardo who was trying to rebuild the column dismantled by the Peci revelations.

On the 26th, the Minister of Justice, Adolfo Sarti, announced the closure of the Asinara prison on the pretext that the decision had already been taken before the D'Urso

Giovanni D'Urso seen while held hostage by the BR. (Open source)

kidnapping.[73] The same day, a revolt broke out in the Trani special prison organised by the BR collective led by Piccioni, Seghetti, Pasquale Abatangelo and Salvatore Ricciardi. An attempted assault by the police was repelled by prisoners who used explosives. In exchange for the lives of the Trani hostages and Judge D'Urso, they demanded the immediate closure of Asinara and the transfer to other prisons of all prisoners held in Trani.[74]

On December 29, the carabinieri *Gruppo d'Intervento Speciale* (Special Intervention Group or GIS) launched a new assault. The prisoners resisted for more than two hours, but they had to surrender and faced reprisals. The BR response was brutal. On 31 December, carabiniere General Enrico Galvaligi, deputy head of the office in charge of monitoring special prisons, was killed in Rome.[75]

Contrary to what happened during the Moro kidnapping, the BR's position, which did not ask for the release of prisoners but only the improvement of their living conditions, appeared reasonable to certain political forces, in particular within the Radical Party. The BR took advantage of this crack in the firmness front, on 4 January to announce D'Urso's death sentence, but they specified that the final decision had to rest with the prisoners' committees. Trani's committee responded on 5 January, saying it considered it possible to suspend the death sentence if a BR statement was published in mainstream media.[76]

A delegation of radical parliamentarians went to Palmi and Trani to receive similar statements from the committees of these prisons. The next day, representatives of the Radical Party went to publish the Trani committee statement in certain newspapers. For his part, a magistrate took responsibility for a gesture of relaxation by freeing the former brigadist Faina, who suffered from cancer, despite criticism from the government.

Finally, on 12 January, the Radicals used their legal television speaking time to let D'Urso's daughter read a declaration begging the newspapers to publish the BR's texts in order to save her father's life. The BR then said they were giving the press 48 hours to bring out statements from the Trani and Palmi committees and organisation documents in exchange for D'Urso's life. Some newspapers, such as *Il Messaggero*, *Il Giorno* and *Secolo XIX*, decided to publish them and D'Urso was finally released on 15 January near the Ministry of Grace and Justice building.[77]

According to Moretti, D'Urso's kidnapping was the most successful BR operation. They succeeded in breaking the firmness front, in dividing the magistrates and in closing the Asinara special prison. But the D'Urso affair quickly emerged as the swansong of an organisation that was inexorably fragmenting. The era of the united BR came to an end, symbolised by the fall of Moretti. The latter, still seeking to save the unity of the organisation, travelled to Milan in early 1981 with Fenzi and Balzerani with the intention of rebuilding a new column after the expulsion of the Alasia column. He reconnected and looked for contacts. Among the latter was Renato Longo, a common criminal formerly a police informant. The latter led the police to the BR chief who was arrested on 4 April with Fenzi.[78]

Established in 1978, the *Gruppo d'Intervento Speciale* (Special Intervention Group) became the special forces unit of the Carabinieri, responsible for counter-terrorism operations and the protection of executives and dignitaries. These GIS operators were photographed during an exercise, together with an Agusta-Bell 212 helicopter. (Albert Grandolini collection)

8
ORGANISATION, TACTICS, ARMAMENT, INTERNATIONAL LINKS

Moretti's arrest brought an era in BR history to a close. Then began the decline of the organisation. It had existed for 10 years, an impressive longevity which had been accompanied since 1974 by an increase in military operations, some spectacular, and which posed a major challenge to the Italian State. The BR's successes, and the resilience they showed in the face of police forces blows, had to first be found within the organisation whose structures had proven to be effective.

The BR's Organisation

It was in 1975 that the BR acquired a definitive structure made up of brigades, columns and fronts.[1] It was an organisation formed for 'movement warfare', endowed with great agility and great mobility, to enable it to adapt to the manoeuvres of the adversary and to avoid encirclement. In 1972, the BR was an underground military organisation operating on the Leninist principle of 'democratic centralism'. The CE and the DS formed the top of its hierarchy. The first brought together representatives of the fronts – between four and five militants – in order to allow efficient centralisation of information and rapid execution of directives. It therefore represented the highest BR operational level. Its mission was to implement the political line defined by the DS, to direct and coordinate the activities of the fronts and the columns and to examine and approve all the military actions of the organisation. Major operations like the Moro kidnapping were directly designed and managed by it. Finally, it was responsible for the administration of the BR's property and patrimony. The central role it played in the organisation aroused criticism and, over time, it appeared to many to be increasingly authoritarian and closed to debate, a situation denounced in 1979 by Curcio and Franceschini.[2]

The DS was the highest political authority. It was a kind of revolutionary council or 'central committee' of 15 to 16 members, in which all the columns and fronts were represented. It met once or twice a year on an ordinary basis, and extraordinarily at the request of a column, a front or the CE. Its mission was to guarantee 'maximum democracy' within the BR but also to control the CE, to define the strategy of the organisation and to modify its structures.[3]

The BR's basic operational unit was the column. In 1972, there were only two, that of Turin and that of Milan, though there would be six at the time of their maximum expansion. Towards the end of the unitary period of the BR, the Neapolitan column and the Tuscan and Sardinian revolutionary committees completed the organisation. The revolutionary committees were located in areas not conducive to armed struggle and played a logistical support role for the nearest columns.

Each column had a central management structure made up of four to five militants, which coordinated the work of the brigades. The column was an essential element of the BR organisation since it acted autonomously over an entire geographical area. It was above all a point of contact between the centralised national structure whose decisions it enforced and the local reality with its own particularities. This articulation between the national and the local gave each column its specificity.

The decision-making and operational autonomy of the columns depended on the type of action planned. At the national level, when

Table 1: BR Columns and Brigades

Area	Column	Brigade
Turin	Column 'Margherita Cagol-Mara'	Nuclei 'Lorenzo Betassa' Brigade 'Presse' (Fiat Mirafiori) Brigade 'Rivalta' Brigade 'Lancia' Brigade 'Lancia' Brigade 'Carrozerie'
Genoa	Column 'Francesco Berardi'	Brigade 'P. Panciarelli-Pasquale' (Italsider) Brigade 'Riccardo Dura-Roberto' (Harbour) Brigade 'Annamaria Ludmann-Cecilia' (Santo Marino)
Milan	Column 'Walter Alasia-Luca'	Brigade 'R. Serafini-Marco' (Alfa Romeo) Brigade 'Walter Pezzoli-Giorgio' (Sesto San Giovanni) Brigade 'Fabrizio Pelli' (Hospitals)
Veneto	Column 'Annamaria Ludmann-Cecilia' (created in 1980)	
Rome	Column '28 March'	Brigade Ospedaliere Brigade Primavalle Brigade Torre Spaccata Brigade Centocelle Brigade Ostia Brigade Tiburtina Brigade SIP Brigade Ferrovieri
Naples		1st extralegal brigade 2nd extralegal brigade Service structure

a campaign was decided upon, the columns surveyed the targets that might fit into the desired objectives. When the column leadership had chosen this target, it submitted it to the CE for consideration if it was a question of committing homicide. For an injury, it sufficed to notify the CE which might possibly exercise a right of veto. The action was implemented by the members of the column and planned by its leadership. It was the direction of the columns which then drafted the leaflets claiming the actions carried out.[4]

Between the columns and the top of the organisation, the national fronts played the fundamental role of coordination and liaison. The Logistics Front appeared to be the most important since it managed all practical problems, that of false documents, housing, bases, weapons and cars. The front of the fight against the counter-revolution was divided between a sector of the police forces, a penitentiary sector and a sector of the working class and factories. It

The BR attacked not only the representatives of the Italian state and NATO, but also political parties. This shows the DC office in Milano after an attack by the BR on 1 April 1980. (Open source)

was responsible for gathering information on these different sectors and studying possible targets. The Mass front divided into the sector of service workers and that of the marginalised proletariat. In the summer of 1980, the prison sector became a front, entrusted to the management of Senzani, whose task was to communicate with the prisoner collectives and the brigades which brought together the imprisoned activists.[5]

If the organisation in column and brigade responded to a vertical logic of organisation, the fronts obeyed a horizontal logic. The connection between the two took place through a complex mechanism. Each column was represented in the fronts but within the columns there was a distribution of tasks according to the division into fronts since they all included a logistics manager or a counter-revolution manager.[6]

At the BR's base, the brigades were made up of different cells, each with three to five people, endowed with 'tactical autonomy' but subject to the strategic line of the organisation. The brigades applied the same principles as the national structure with a hierarchy and strict compartmentalisation in order to ensure their efficiency and safety at all levels.[7]

From the mid-1970s, satellite organisations appeared around the BR. This was particularly the case in Genoa with the Buranello Brigade, formed in November 1979, to which belonged an irregular brigadist who failed to convince his comrades to join the BR. If the Buranello Brigade remained autonomous, it carried out modest actions, such as fires, whose targets were identical to those of the BR. It openly affirmed its solidarity with them and provided them bases. Finally, at Balzerani's request, the Buranello Brigade joined the BR in the spring of 1981. The Bolzaneto Struggle Committee was founded at the end of 1976 before being joined by Leonardo Bertulazzi who was a member of the BR. The committee then became a support group for the BR, while maintaining its operational autonomy. It led small actions, the most important of which were attacks on carabinieri barracks. The committee became the 28 March brigade after the Via Fracchia event.[8]

The operating principle on which all the BR structures were based was compartmentalisation, that was to say the ignorance of everything that did not fall within its area of intervention. It was considered an essential element for the survival and the smooth running of the organisation. Compartmentalisation was based on secrecy, not only towards those outside the organisation but also within the BR where activists were excluded from information and ignored anything outside their sector. It was both vertical between the various authorities at all levels and horizontal between the columns, the fronts and the brigades. The fragmentation of information was counterbalanced by the omniscience of the governing bodies who controlled all decisions and had an overview of the organisation. It was up to the CE to ensure that compartmentalisation did not limit dialogue and prevent political debate, a task that had become increasingly difficult over time.

At the time of their maximum expansion, the BR had a structure which had enabled them to achieve many successes in the armed struggle against the state. It was not a pyramidal formation, but a complex set of organs dependent on each other and connected to perform different functions simultaneously. Despite the arrests, it managed to resist over time and implement sometimes spectacular actions. However, its growing centralisation was gradually eliminating the spirit of initiative and the autonomy of militants and brigades as the link with the working-class world was unravelling. This trend was largely the result of the initial choice in favour of underground and compartmentalisation.

Life in the BR

In 1975, when the BR redefined their strategic line, they also specified the means to achieve it. Clandestinity then became the indispensable condition for the survival of a politico-military organisation operating within the metropolises, but this condition should not prevent militants from operating within the working class. From a tactical point of view, it allowed them to gain the advantage over an adversary forced to live exposed. Going underground was therefore not considered a defensive but an offensive tactic.[9]

The clandestinity principles led to the division of the BR forces into two types of militants, the regulars and the irregulars. They were all considered essential but with different roles. Regulars were 'professional revolutionaries' who devoted all of their time to the organisation. The vast majority had severed their ties with the law and their ordinary social life to go underground. On the contrary, the irregulars if they worked in an underground organisation, lived a legal life. Their task was to gain the broadest popular support for BR politics and help the regulars. From a political point of view, the BR did not differentiate between regular and irregular militants, who had the same rights and duties within the organisation, so much so even an irregular could be part of the DS. They were nevertheless excluded from the leadership of the fronts, the columns or the CE, where only illegals could work.

The life of the brigadists was governed by the respect of many rules which were recorded in a manual entitled *Standards of Behaviour*, found in a Pavia base. The activist should not go to a meeting without someone else in the organisation knowing. New contacts should be discussed with the column leaders and organised according to a predetermined pattern. Each activist had meeting places but had to avoid repeating meetings in the same places. Regulars should not take notes but memorise everything they need to know; notebooks with phone numbers, names or addresses were prohibited. The use of phones, which could be monitored, was limited to short communications and only in emergency situations.

Regarding the use of cars, they had to have all the necessary legal documents, contain nothing that could attract the attention of passers-by, thieves and even police forces. When travelling in the city, it was necessary to drive safely to avoid any accident, to respect the highway code and to be careful not to be followed.[10]

The bases were also managed according to precise rules. Each base was frequented exclusively by the militants who lived there and known only by another member previously designated by the column. The access road to the base had to be easy to control which means that the base had to be quite isolated, far from bars, public places or shops. The residents in the BR's bases had to build an ordinary social facade that was credible vis-à-vis neighbours, in particular by respecting plausible schedules depending on whether they claimed to be a worker, employee or civil servant. In order to go unnoticed, the activist had to dress in an ordinary way and be neat in appearance.[11] Again, it was about going unnoticed, not letting anything appear that could attract attention, especially from police forces.

All brigadists used a nom de guerre within the organisation for reasons of compartmentalisation. In theory, therefore, no one should know the real identity of another activist, but in practice this was not the case, especially for the leaders such as Moretti, Morucci, Faranda, Balzerani and Micaletto. Their faces were well known for having been featured numerous times in the newspapers and often they crossed paths in far-left circles before entering the BR. Normally, an irregular should know only two or three faces in a column. However, compartmentalisation worked since some activists had never, to this day, been identified despite the confessions of the repenters.

The lives of regulars, who were very often illegals, unfolded almost exclusively within the organisation. They had to cut all ties with their loved ones and their families. Moretti thus abandoned his wife and son in 1972 and did not see them again until in prison in the 1980s. This resulted in the formation of couples within the BR, the best known being those of Morucci and Faranda, and of Moretti and Balzerani. In order to survive, the regulars received a salary which, in 1979, was 250,000 lire,[12] which was modest, but their housing was covered by the organisation as well as the costs that they could justify. The latter could also pay money to the families of regulars and who bore the costs of lawyers in the event of an arrest.[13]

Those who wanted to join the BR were first put in contact with irregulars who were responsible for testing them, sometimes for months on end, through political discussions. Then they came into contact with a regular. They only knew those with whom they distributed leaflets or carried out an action before returning to their normal life. Gradually, they were integrated into the organisation and took part in more dangerous actions. Thus, Massimo Cianfanelli met Gallinari, the Roman column leader, at the end of 1978. The latter asked him to write a document on the universities, then to follow a professor, and then to locate the military antennae in the region of Rome. Finally, he was invited to a weapons training session before participating in the assassination of Magistrate Tartaglione.[14]

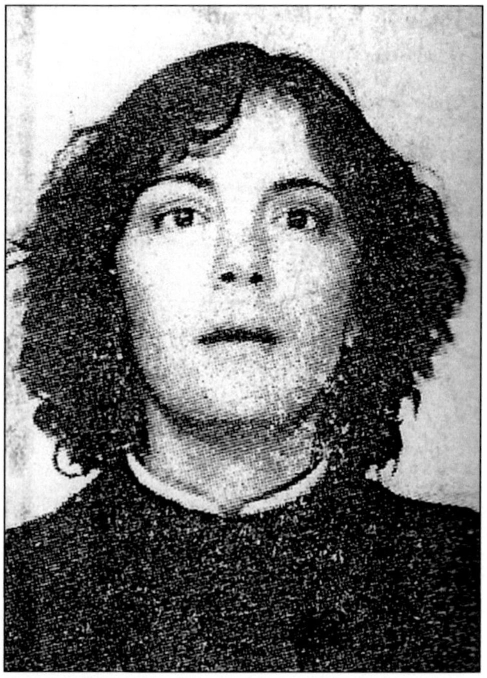

Barbara Balzerani shown in a photograph taken on her arrest. (Open source)

In the event of arrest, activists had to declare themselves a political prisoner, refuse to answer questions and above all, they ceased to play a leading role in the BR. Leaving the organisation was also possible and relatively easy. Many did so without suffering consequences, on the sole condition of remaining discreet. Thus, Germano Maccari, who took part in Moro's imprisonment with a very important function, left the BR immediately after 9 May, continuing to live in his neighbourhood for years. Morucci and Faranda did the same. Peci also cited the case of Rafaelle Pisano, an activist who left the organisation after a few months.[15]

The numbers of regulars were small. According to Franceschini, in 1971 the BR had only three underground militants, a hundred irregulars and about a thousand sympathisers.[16] Moretti estimated that in the Roman group he led in 1978 there were no more than 10 regulars and no fewer than six. According to him, also, there were never more than 10 underground militants per column.[17] In 1978, therefore, there were about 120 illegals who formed the backbone of the organisation, as they passed regularly from one column or from one front to another. It was a format that appeared to be reduced, but the support for the BR was much broader and the organisation relied on a circle of sympathisers who sometimes had entered, more or less convinced in the organisation, to leave it a few months later, often after their first violent action, but while remaining in the zone of contiguity with the armed struggle. They provided occasional help which could prove to be invaluable. This was the case of Patrizia Lucidi, typist at the secretariat of the Under-Secretary of State for the Interior.[18] In Milan, Mario Bondesan, a former partisan, hid weapons at his home and sheltered illegals like Moretti, Franceschini and Peci.[19] Moretti says he spent most of his life underground lodging in sympathisers' houses.[20] In this circle of sympathisers there were also BR lawyers like Edoardo Arnaldi who, according to Peci, was paid by the organisation and conveyed messages between it and the prisoners.[21]

For Moretti, the number of BR activists corresponded globally to that of arrests, that is, 911 from 1970 to the beginning of the 1990s.[22] He added that you have to multiply this number by 10 to get an idea of the number of supporters who provided aid to BR,[23] or about 10,000, a considerable number. Maccari gave even higher figures. According to him, there were 3,000 to 4,000 regulars and irregulars and between 30,000 and 40,000 sympathisers.[24] The US administration gave lower figures. It estimated that there were a thousand organised activists and 2,000 external supporters in 1978–1979, figures which dropped to 100 organised activists and 200 supporters in 1982–1983.[25] These latest figures reveal that from the beginning of the 1980s, the circle of sympathisers disappeared, leaving around the BR a sort of desert that many activists speak of in their memoirs.

International Links

According to the repenter, the BR tried to establish links with the West German RAF very early on, and it was thanks to this that the Italians came into contact with the Palestinians.[26] In fact, until 1972, the BR's relations with foreign organisations were the work of Fetrinelli. When he died, contact with the outside world seemed to be cut off. According to Christian Jansen, relations between the BR and the RAF did not begin until the early 1980s. He argued that the BR in the 1970s only had contact with the 2 June Movement.[27] However, it seems that contact with the RAF was established in 1978 with the arrival of German militants in Milan. They were then entrusted to Azzolini until his arrest and then to Moretti.

Despite the ideological proximity, there were many differences between the two organisations. While the RAF was made up mostly of intellectuals and students, the sociological profile of the BR was more varied with many workers and employees. This difference was reflected ideologically by the loyalty to Marxism-Leninism of the BR while the Germans were more libertarian. The BR did not fail to reproach the RAF for its lack of integration into the working class. Savasta also confirmed the negative judgment of the BR on the RAF, too committed to the struggle against US imperialism and NATO and its alignment with the USSR foreign policy positions which manifested itself in the renunciation of denouncing the 'Soviet social-imperialism.'[28] There was no operational cooperation between Germans and Italians and relations were limited solely to exchanges of false papers or money.[29]

According to Franceschini, at the time of the CPM, Simioni would have contact with the French *Gauche prolétarienne* and *Vive la Révolution*.[30] It was not until 1978 that the organisation decided to establish relations with other fighting formations in Europe. For that, brigadists went to Paris where there were already militants who fled Italy. Moretti thus travelled to France from 1978 to 1981, often accompanied by Anna Laura Braghetti who spoke French. They met independent French activists but avoided Irish Republican Army (IRA) activists with whom they felt they had little in common. According to Peci, the BR had supplied a load of P38 pistols to the French NAPAP (*Noyaux armés pour l'autonomie populaire* or Armed Nuclei for Popular Autonomy).[31] Relations were deeper with Basque ETA but did not lead to anything concrete.

The BR had links with the West German RAF and as the latter was linked to the East German *Ministerium für Staatssicherheit* (Ministry for State Security or *Stasi*), the question of the links between the brigadists and the socialist countries cannot be avoided. Certain elements showed a convergence of analyses between them. The CPSU leaders were hostile to the PCI policy which wanted to take power by peaceful means. As early as 1973, Boris Ponomarev, secretary of the CPSU Central Committee for International Relations, regretted that the Italian comrades were not interested in preparing for armed struggle. The criticism continued in the following years especially as an SED document indicated that the Soviets believed that the situation in Italy was ripe for a decisive offensive.[32]

Gianluca Falanga has written the most serious study on *Stasi*-BR links.[33] He shows that until the Moro kidnapping, East Berlin completely ignored the BR. After Moro's death, the *Stasi* tried to find out if there were links between East German citizens and brigadists.[34] It discovered that Pietro Morlacchi, who was a political refugee in the GDR from 1965 to 1968, was married to Heidi Peusch, an East German citizen. In 1977, the *Stasi* had already taken an interest in the latter because of its links with the RAF entourage. When at the end of 1979, Peusch applied for a visa to see her parents in East Germany, the *Stasi* considered taking the opportunity to obtain information on the BR, but ultimately the political leadership rejected this option. Subsequently, the *Stasi* was mainly interested in the links between the BR and the RAF.[35] Finally, at no time was there any direct support or collaboration between the *Stasi* and the BR, or even meetings.

Czechoslovakia had long been suspected of having maintained close ties with the BR. In 1968, Jan Sejna deserted the Czechoslovak People's Army and joined the CIA. He then allegedly declared that military training camps organised by Moscow on Czechoslovak soil had existed since 1964. In these camps, members of the Italian far-left such as Feltrinelli, Viel from the *XXII Ottobre* group or Negri from *Autonomia Operaia* would have received training.[36] He did not cite any brigadist's name but his testimony related to the period prior to 1968, when the BR did not yet exist. The suspicion of collusion between the latter and the *Státní Bezpečnost* (State Security or *StB*) remained so high that in 1975 the PCI leadership sent a representative to Prague to ask the Czechoslovaks to cease all contact with the BR.[37] However, research carried out by Fernando Orlandi in the Prague archives shows that there was no relationship between the BR and Czechoslovakia.[38]

The parliamentary commission of inquiry into the Mitrokhin affair, formed in 2002 under the Berlusconi government, argued in its final report that there was a link between the KGB and the BR through the notorious terrorist Ilich Ramirez Sanchez, alias Carlos. But this assertion was not based, again, on any convincing evidence.[39] A 1980 KGB memorandum, found in the Bulgarian security services archives, even shows that the Soviets had only superficial knowledge of the BR. If it is possible that the documents proving the collusion of the socialist countries with the BR have been destroyed or are not yet accessible to the public, their current absence confirms the assertion of the historian Victor Zaslavsky: 'As long as a specific documentation is not available on the subject, the attempt to explain Italian terrorism as a phenomenon directed from abroad does not seem to have any basis.'[40]

The BR's most extensive foreign relations were with the Palestinians. The Palestinian movement welcomed the weakening of the United States' Mediterranean allies. It supplied weapons while the BR offered assistance with false papers and as political and logistical support.[41] In 1979, the BR thus carried out an operation planned for a long time in collaboration with the Palestinian Liberation Organization (PLO). It consisted of travelling to Lebanon to take delivery of a large shipment of weapons, part of which was destined for the IRA. The PLO thus sought to strengthen organisations considered anti-imperialist. Mario Moretti, Riccardo Dura, Massimo Gidoni, a doctor from Ancona, owner of the sailboat *Papago* and a Venetian, sailed from Ancona to Greece at the end of the summer. The weapons delivery took place off the coast of Tripoli in Lebanon, then the sailboat returned to Venice where the weapons were unloaded.[42]

Antonio Savasta who, together with Emilia Libera, was recruited by Bruno Seghetti. (Author's collection)

Nevertheless, nothing suggests that the BR was operationally involved in Palestinian armed activities in Italy or abroad or that BR militants were trained in Palestinian camps. Especially, the Palestinian organisations had no influence on the political line of the Italians. These distant relations could be explained in part by the agreement that the Palestinians made with Rome. They promised not to commit military actions on Italian soil or against Italian targets. In exchange, the Italian government turned a blind eye to their clandestine activities on its territory.[43] In order not to break this agreement, the Palestinians therefore refused too much collaboration with the BR. If the Popular Front for the Liberation of Palestine, embodying the Marxist wing of the PLO, directly supported the BR by delivering them arms, Yasser Arafat did not hesitate to denounce them. They were for him 'agents of imperialism'. The BR was always worried about the risk of being manipulated by international sponsors and thus kept their focus on the Italian sociopolitical context.[44]

BR Armament and Tactics

Brigadists generally had no military experience when they joined the organisation. The BR therefore tried to provide them with at least some training in weapons handling, but Moretti admitted that it was reduced and only occurred in preparation for an operation. This training was made even more difficult by the urban establishment of the BR. To remedy this problem, the brigadists left the towns to join the surrounding countryside. Patrizio Peci of the Milanese column told how shooting training took place in the caves of Crissolo in Piedmont[45] while the members of the Roman column trained in the Apennines, in isolated places, country trails or caves, and the Genoese column carried out training on the Righi mountains.[46] These shooting sessions were nevertheless limited and Moretti adds that during the 10 years that he was a member of the organisation, he only fired twice with a machine gun.[47] Regarding the BR's most successful operation, the Moro kidnapping, Gallinari says it was only simulated once, in Vetrelli, during a DS meeting.[48]

Patrizio Peci, of the Turin Red Brigades, seen during his trial. (Open source)

Despite their poor knowledge of firearms and the dangers of their use, the BR had always refused to use explosives in their actions. They wrote on this subject that 'It is not difficult to see that the use of dynamite generally has the effect of indiscriminately terrorising the masses, and not just the enemy. It also lends itself to the most disparate interpretations, on the right-wing and on the left-wing, given the frequent use that the reaction has made of it.'[49] This refusal to carry out bombings was explained for Moretti by the desire of the BR to take care that their actions did not affect 'civilians'. For the Moro kidnapping, they refused to allow the operation to take place in the church in Piazza dei Giuochi Delfici because there were many children around.[50]

When DS set the BR's orientation, this translated militarily into the organisation of a campaign that became the frame of reference for tactical actions. At the base, the fronts and the columns sought objectives and ensured the possibility of achieving them by carrying out surveillance actions. They then proposed to the CE to carry out military operations by providing it with information on the targets, their habits and the modalities of action. It was the CE that decided whether the operation should be carried out or not. If, on the tactical level, an operation had to meet three criteria, the element of surprise, security and military superiority, its implementation generally revolved around three cells, that of attack, that of cover and that of support. The attack cell took action. It was often made up of at least two brigadists, but this number varied according to the importance of the chosen target. The cover cell was close to the objective so that it could intervene if the attack cell failed or to deal with an unexpected threat. The support cell had vehicles to allow the evacuation of all brigadists.[51]

Usually, the BR commando struck their victims as they moved from their home to their place of work or vice versa, most often in front of their point of departure or arrival, more rarely, en route. For a kill or an injury, the attack cell approached the victim and shot an entire magazine at them. A strict rule was imposed during the actions, no contact should be made with the victim, no words should be said. This rule was part of one of the basic strategies for depersonalising the enemy. The target to be hit thus became a symbol that was not the object of pity, hatred or any other feeling. After the action, the brigadists fled as quickly as possible.

Some actions followed different tactical patterns. This was the case in the actions against Professors Peschiera and Cuocolo by the Genoese column. Against Peschiera, the operation unfolded like a real military attack. The four brigadists entered the higher formation school. They immobilised the five other people present and locked them in a cupboard. They placed a sign around the professor's neck and, before leaving, they shot him in the legs. Professor Cuocolo

A police checkpoint in Torino in 1980. In reaction to BR's attacks, by this time police officers were better equipped than at earlier times – including ballistic vests and Baretta M12 submachine guns. (Albert Grandolini collection)

was also injured in the legs in a courtroom in front of his students. These actions were a mix of different types of BR operations: the leg injuries, the military assault on a 'den of the counter-revolution' as was the case with the attack on the DC regional headquarters in Piazza Nicosia, with the sign attached to the victim as during the first kidnappings carried out by the organisation.[52]

In supplying the BR with weapons, Moretti says they never used, with one exception, organised crime or arms trafficking networks. More than revolutionary morality, it was rather the awareness that this traffic was monitored by the authorities that explained this choice. According to him, the BR obtained weapons in three different ways. Some were bought from armouries by activists who presented false documents, others were weapons dating from the Second World War and kept by former partisans.[53] The last method came from links with foreign organisations.

Foreign supply chains were varied. According to Prefect Coronas, the BR received weapons from the Swiss anarchist group AKO which stole them from the depots of the Swiss army.[54] The delivery of arms in Lebanon in 1979 included around 150 Sterling submachine guns with two magazines each, around 10 Belgian FALs, two light machine guns of Russian or Chinese manufacture, six rocket grenades, two boxes of hand grenades of pineapple type, five or six quintals of plastic explosives, 20 Energa anti-tank grenades, electric detonators and fuses, 9mm ammunition and 25 surface-to-air missiles.[55] But only Sterling submachine guns and anti-tank grenades were distributed to the various BR columns while the rest of the cargo, destined for the IRA, was hidden in Sardinia.[56] According to Savasta, PLO arms deliveries also came from France.[57]

The BR arsenal had always been modest. During the attack on Via Fani, the commando had two FNAB-43 submachine guns dating from the Second World War and their most modern weapons were a Beretta M12 and a Skorpion. Buonavita, in 1982, explained that the 'fantasy of super-sophisticated BR weaponry strikes me as really ridiculous.'[58] Nevertheless, Peci asserted that the Roman column had at the time of Moro's kidnapping 'Belgian FAL machine gun, five or six Sterling machine guns, a Soviet A.M. assault gun, and pistols of various types, among which were a Beretta 81 and a Browning H.P. 9 calibres long, with a two-row loader.'[59]

The BR's operation required a lot of money to buy or rent housing, procure weapons, and finance the illegals. The organisation was financed first by thefts that activists called 'expropriations'. Moretti says that in order to keep the organisation alive there must be monthly attack on a bank whose money was handed over to the CE, which then distributed it to the columns and the fronts. These operations were not without risk, as on 8 October 1975, when a commando from the Genoese column attacked the Savings Bank of Genoa and Imperia and stole 120 million lire. As the brigadists left the bank, they ran into two carabinieri and a shoot-out broke out. They managed to flee but one of them was nevertheless injured.[60] To avoid these dangerous actions which required time and militants while the financial needs continued to increase, the BR decided in 1975 to proceed with the kidnapping of a rich industrialist and chose Gancia, but the operation was a failure and cost Mara Cagol her life.[61] Pierino Costa's kidnapping in Genoa in 1977 was a success. It allowed the BR to obtain a ransom of one and a half billion lire which protected them from financial needs until 1981.[62]

Table 2: Attacks claimed by the BR from 1970 to 1980[63]

Year	Attacks	Deaths	Injuries
1970	4		
1971	6		
1972	28		
1973	7		
1974	25	3	
1975	30	1	3
1976	53	6	2
1977	56	3	20
1978	106	16	18
1979	66	10	15
1980	59	16	10
Total	440	55	68

9
DEFEAT, 1981–1988

With Moretti's arrest, the last of the BR's founders disappeared. The organisation was fracturing, and splits multiplied during the 1980s, weakening it even more. The Italian State continued its policy of destroying the BR and gaining victories in this fight. The agony of the BR would not end until the end of the decade, however.

The Four Kidnappings of 1981

During the winter of 1981, the BR, including the Alasia column, jointly decided to carry out a series of kidnappings. However, each of the operations was carried out independently by the different columns, which marginalised the CE. The first to be kidnapped was Ciro Cirillo, on 27 April 1981, by the Neapolitan column, now merged with the Prison Front and led by Senzani. On 20 May, the director of the Montedison company, Giuseppe Taliercio, was kidnapped by the Venetian column. On 3 June an Alfa Romeo executive, Renzo Sandrucci was kidnapped by the Alasia column and a week later in San Benedetto del Tronto, the Prison Front kidnapped Roberto Peci, Patrizio's brother. At that time, none of the other three hostages had yet been released.

The Cirillo kidnapping was symbolic of the political line followed by the Neapolitan column, led by Senzani since the summer of 1980, and wanted to address the marginal proletariat notably through the question of housing and work. For this, it proposed to form a 'guerrilla party' capable of recognising the historical function of the working class as a revolutionary class, but also of representing the new demands of the popular classes, the unemployed, prisoners and the marginalised.[1]

On 27 April, a BR commando led by Senzani arrived in a van in front of Cirillo's house in Torre del Greco in the province of Naples. Vincenzo Stuttgart parked the vehicle in front of Cirillo's garage and waited with Enzo Olivieri and Emilio Manna hidden inside. Antonio Chiocchi hid near the pavement in front of the house, while Giovanni Planzio and Vittorio Bolognese stood in front of the garage entrance. When Cirillo's car entered the garage, Planzio and Bolognese followed it inside. They first shot the escort agent Luigi Carbone, who, although injured, reacted by rushing at Planzio, but was hit by Bolognese who intervened to help his comrade and was ultimately killed by submachine gun-fire from Senzani. Cirillo's driver, Mario Cancello, then tried to close the garage door which had remained open, but his movement was noticed by Planzio who, fearing that it was an attempt to recover a weapon, killed him suddenly. Senzani and Planzio entered the car to capture Cirillo who while defending himself was struck with a gun butt, then was dragged outside and pushed into the van. Cirillo's secretary, Ciro Fiorillo, who stood motionless, was injured in the legs. Meanwhile, Chiocchi cut the telephone wires in an attempt to isolate the area but was unable to prevent the Cirillo family from calling for help. The van left, followed by a Fiat 128 car with Manna and Bolognese and then stopped at an isolated location near Herculaneum. Cirillo was transferred to a Fiat 126 driven by Pasquale Aprea and then taken to Cercola where he was locked in a cage built inside a house.[2]

Roberto Peci in the hands of the BR. (Author's collection)

If Cirillo, regional councillor for town planning and economic construction of the Campania region, was a secondary political figure, he was vice-president of the technical committee for the reconstruction of Campania after the earthquake of 1980 and therefore managed considerable public money. His kidnapping took place at a time of strong social tensions in the Neapolitan region which were reflected in protests by the homeless and the unemployed. Thus, on 25 April, two days before the kidnapping, the homeless in Salerno blocked the railway, preventing the passage of trains.

The conditions for the release of the hostage by the BR took up the demands of the homeless by asking for the requisition of vacant housing, the closure of the caravan village installed at the Oltremare Fair and for unemployment benefits. The DC was showing signs of firmness at the start but reiterated that it was ready to respond to the most urgent needs of the population. To support these demands, on 15 May the Neapolitan column wounded the DC municipal councillor Rosario Giovine and the communist councillor for town planning of the municipality of Naples, Umberto Siola.[3] On the 22nd of the same month, this time in Rome, it was the Provincial Employment Office director who was injured, followed a week

Ciro Cirillo seen while held hostage by the Brigate Rosse. (Author's collection)

later, on the 29th, by Professor Giuseppe Magagna, employed in a professional formation centre of a Salesian institute.[4]

If the DC refused to negotiate for Moro, it agreed to do so for Cirillo. The Neapolitan column was favourable to negotiation and even to accepting money to finance its political project of a guerrilla party. These negotiations included both the secret service and organised crime. The head of the Camorra, Raffaele Cutolo, detained at Ascoli Piceno prison offered himself as mediator in exchange for improving his conditions of detention. On 20 May, his lieutenant, Pasquale D'Amico, asked the BR to release Cirillo and then to leave Campania. After a few days, on 26 May, the head of the DC group in the city council declared that while awaiting the completion of the construction of new buildings, the vacant houses could be requisitioned. On the 29th, the mayor of Naples signed the decree for the requisition and unemployment benefit for young people aged 18 to 29, which were paid from 2 June.[5]

However, Cirillo still remained a prisoner for a month. On 18 June, a large ransom of about one and a half billion lire was paid, collected by the friends of Cirillo, but this was not enough for his release, because the BR demanded the publication of their documents in the newspapers. On 9 July, they announced the hostage's death sentence. Finally, on 24 July, Cirillo was released. A few years later, Judge Carlo Alemi, during the investigation of the case, came to the conviction that Cirillo was released after a complex negotiation. According to two repenters, Pasquale Aprea and Maria Rosaria Perna, the BR learnt in early May that the Camorra offered 5 billion lire for the life of the hostage, as well as weapons and information on magistrates and men who fought against terrorism. After a moment of resistance, Senzani succeeded in convincing the Neapolitan column leaders to accept this offer.[6]

The BR CE was not satisfied with the progress and especially with the conclusion of Cirillo's kidnapping. The obscure and murky nature of the hostage's release negotiations raised doubts that needed to be discussed in a meeting between it and the Neapolitan column leader. But the latter decided not to respond to the invitation. This further widened the gap that already existed between the CE and Senzani.[7]

Giuseppe Taliercio, director of the Montedison petrochemical plant in Marghera, was designated as a target by the CE. The direction of the Venetian column entrusted the investigation to Savasta, Marina Bono, Gianni Francescutti and Cesare Di Lenardo. The BR saw Taliercio as a symbol of the layoffs, ongoing corporate restructuring and environmental problems brought on by Montedison. Above all, the Venetian column was at the time the only column loyal to the CE capable of organising and managing a major military action. On the morning of 20 May 1981, four brigadists, Savasta, Lo Bianco, Pietro Vanzi and Francescutti, in Guardia di Finanza uniforms, entered Taliercio's house and kidnapped him, after having immobilised his wife and their children. The hostage was taken to a house, guarded by Giovanna Massa. Throughout the operation, the commando was flanked by other brigadists acting as cover.[8]

The hostage was held prisoner in Tercento, a small town in Friuli, under a tent in the attic of a thatched cottage. During his imprisonment, Taliercio was questioned but he refused to collaborate. For his release, the BR asked Montedison to waive the layoffs, but they received no response or request to open negotiations. On 26 June, they announced the hostage's death sentence. On 3 July, the CE, then composed of Novelli, Savasta, Lo Bianco and Balzerani, decided on the execution. On 5 July, Talierco was informed that he would be released soon, but was shot 16 times and his body was abandoned near the petrochemical plant. While

Giuseppe Taliercio while held hostage by the BR. (Open source)

the BR claimed his death, the Prison Front condemned the murder. Above all, it provoked the protest of many workers and there were thus 60,000 who denounced the BR during a demonstration in the industrial city of Mestre.[9]

Renzo Sandrucci, head of Alfa Romeo's work organisation office since 1976, was kidnapped on 3 June by the Alasia column. This action was the culmination of the campaign to stop the company restructuring. The Alasia column had already struck in February, when a foreman from Breda in Fucine, Salvatore Compare, was briefly kidnapped, but this was a demonstration action, followed soon after by the murder of Dr Luigi Francesco Marangoni, medical director of the Milan polyclinic. On 12 March, Alberto Valenzasca, Alfa Romeo's Arese foreman was also injured.[10]

The Sandrucci kidnapping was nonetheless condemned by the unions who organised a two-day strike against terrorism and the dismissals on 12 and 19 June. Beyond Sandrucci's fate, the unions feared having been infiltrated by the BR and above all they were worried about the sympathy enjoyed by the brigadists as illustrated by a ten-metre-long BR banner placed in the factory, without anyone being able to indicate the perpetrators. Sandrucci's terms of release, mainly the end of the layoffs, were released on 10 July with photos of the hostage.

Contrary to what happened with Taliercio, negotiations were initiated and Sandrucci was allowed to contact people deemed capable of satisfying the BR's demands, including the director of Radio Popolare and, on several occasions, the Alfa Romeo management. On 7 July, two days after the discovery of Talierco's body, Sandrucci's family held a press conference during which they asked to negotiate his release. Finally, Sandrucci was released after

Cesare di Lenardo (centre) seen during his trial. (Author's collection)

50 days of imprisonment in front of the Magneti Marelli factory, on 23 July 1981.[11]

Roberto Peci, former member of the Marches revolutionary committee, was kidnapped on 10 June 1981 in San Benedetto del Tronto. The action, carried out by the Prison Front and the Neapolitan column without the authorisation of the CE, was part of the campaign against the phenomenon of repentance and collaboration with the police since Roberto was suspected of being an informant. The main reason for his kidnapping, however, remained his brother, Patrizio, who had become the symbol of betrayal. A few days later, moreover, on 19 June, the Prison Front tried to kill Patrizio's lawyer, Antonio De Vita, but the latter reacted by shooting, managing to hit a brigadist, Natalia Ligas.[12]

Senzani and his group were convinced that Patrizio Peci had been arrested the first time, and had agreed to collaborate with Dalla Chiesa before being released and then arrested again with Micaletto. According to the Prison Front, his brother Roberto was also involved in this plot. For the rest of the organisation, Roberto told the carabinieri that his brother called his mother every now and then and during one of these phone calls, Patrizio was reportedly spotted by the carabinieri. Roberto, at the hands of the Prison Front, at first denied his involvement in the case, but then decided to admit it, to save his life, by writing an open letter in which he reconstituted his brother's arrest in light of Senzani's accusations. Roberto Peci was finally shot against a wall on 3 August, after 54 days of imprisonment, in a Roman suburb near the Capannelle racecourse. A red sheet with the BR star and a sign with the words 'Death to traitors' were left beside the corpse.[13] Peci's death appeared to many not as a political act but one of private revenge similar to that of the Mafia, as his interrogation and execution were filmed and photographed to instil fear among the repenters. It appeared to be an act of cruel madness among the brigadists.

The four kidnappings of 1981 created an image of the BR as still powerful and with operational capabilities at their zenith. They were nevertheless the indicators of an organisation in the midst of a crisis. The Neapolitan column and Prison Front played its own score. It negotiated Cirillo's release with the Camorra and the Secret Service for a heavy ransom without reporting to the CE, and then completely independently decided upon and carried out the kidnapping and murder of Roberto Peci. For its part, the Walter Alasia column was taking advantage of Sandrucci's kidnapping to defend the priority it gave to workers' struggles and to criticise the populist deviations of the Neapolitan column and the Prison Front. The unity of the BR then became a memory even if an official split was not announced.

The Dozier Kidnapping

The negotiations for Cirillo's release and the tragic end of Roberto Peci made Senzani's position in the BR difficult. In the summer, the CE, formed by Savasta, Balzerani, Lo Bianco and Novelli, met Senzani but the latter did not wish to avoid the rupture.[14] After the exclusion of the Alasia column in 1980, the Roman and Venetian columns and some Turin and Genoese militants who wanted to maintain the traditional BR line took note of the split with the Neapolitans and decided, in December, to take the name of *Brigate Rosse-Partito Comunista Combattente* (Red Brigades- Communist Combatant Party or BR-PCC).

Within the BR-PCC, the Roman column was the only one practically intact after Moretti's arrest. It had experienced leaders while the Venetian column was led by Balzerani, Lo Bianco and Savasta. The latter, however, was not immune to divisions and while the majority remained within the BR-PCC, a part joined Senzani and prepared an attack on Rovigo prison, from where they would release Suzanna Ronconi and three other activists. A third group formed the 2 August column.

In order to revive the organisation, the CE decided to mobilise a significant part of these forces for a hitherto unprecedented action, the kidnapping of American General James Lee Dozier, Deputy Chief Of Staff for logistics and administration of the command of the Allied land forces in Southern Europe, installed in Verona since June 1981.[15] So far, the BR's actions against NATO and the Americans had been modest, mostly confined to burning consular posts or cars. With the operation against Dozier, the BR engaged in an anti-imperialist strategy chosen by the DS in November 1981 when Washington decided to deploy Pershing II and cruise nuclear missiles in Western Europe, notably in Sicily. It was also possible that the BR, who until then had denounced the socialist camp as imperialist in the same way as the Western camp, sought by attacking NATO, to receive the support of forces favourable to the USSR, in particular the PCI.[16]

In October 1981, BR-PCC leaders decided to launch spectacular action against capitalism and imperialism. Balzerani said, 'The time has come. We always knew that sooner or later we would have to face our main enemy directly. The Americans are increasingly militarising the country. Did you see them placing nuclear missiles in Sicily, in Comiso? We must send out a strong signal. Send a message to other fighting formations in Europe. We must kidnap an American serviceman.'[17] According to Savasta, the brigadists were then aware that the state would react without restraint.

At the end of October, the CE identified a target, General William Cooney, commander of the US Air Force in Vicenza. But after a few weeks of surveillance, this target was abandoned because Cooney had an escort, and his movements were unpredictable. At a new meeting in Milan, the CE decided to kidnap James Dozier, who was placed under surveillance by brigadists who had come from Rome to reinforce the Venetian column. Dozier had regular habits and was not escorted; he was the ideal target and the method of his kidnapping was the same as that for Taliercio.

The action was performed by the Venetian column. On 17 December 1981, Savasta and Pietro Vanzi, disguised as plumbers, arrived at the door of the General's apartment, joined shortly after by Marcello Capuano and Cesare Di Lenardo who followed behind

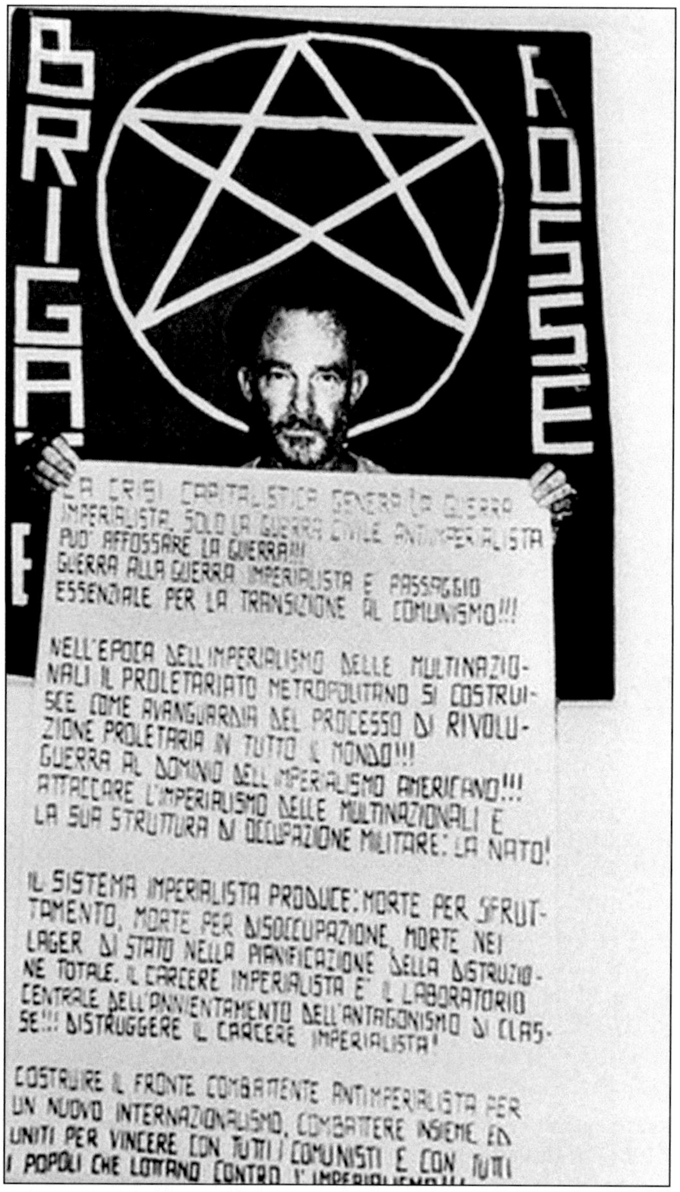

Dozier being held by the BR. (Author's collection)

with a trunk. In the street, Emilia Libera and Ermanno Faggiani were in cover with machine guns and walkie-talkies to communicate with the attack cell. Ruggero Volinia, meanwhile, waited in the van that was supposed to take Dozier away. Once inside the apartment, the brigadists drew their weapons. The General's wife was locked in a cupboard, jewellery was stolen, and Dozier was locked in a wooden box and then transported in the van to Emanuela Fascella's house, on Via Pindemonte in Padua, where he was imprisoned in a tent. According to Dozier, the BR's objectives were to secure the release of prisoners linked to Palestinian terrorism, and the RAF and the BR were to obtain information from him about an alleged plan developed by NATO to control Italian military and economic activities.[18]

Dozier's kidnapping placed the Italian government, chaired by Republican Giovanni Spadolini, in an embarrassing position towards a powerful ally and pushed it to respond to the challenge by short-term suspension of constitutional guarantees. The United States was indeed putting great pressure on Italy to adopt an uncompromising attitude towards the BR. Washington also wanted the case to be handled by Dalla Chiesa, known and respected in American embassy circles. Eventually, the US State Department sent a team of counter-terrorism experts to the scene.[19] Italian authorities

Dozier (left), his daughter and wife (right side of the photograph) with the Italian president Pertini after his rescue by the NOCS. (Open source)

also received support from a US Army Intelligence Support Activity SIGINT unit.[20]

Operation Dozier was operationally poorly planned. Savasta, who led the attack group, did not take the necessary compartmentalisation measures and used bases known to brigadists in jail, as well as sympathisers from backgrounds easily identified by the carabinieri. The latter had a track since Michele Galati, detained in Cuneo prison after his arrest in December 1980, began to collaborate with the police. His information led to the arrest of Volinia, who, certainly under torture, indicated the place where Dozier was.

An NOCS group, equipped with balaclavas, blue camouflage uniforms, ropes, weapons and a ram, then left Rome for Padua where, on Via Pindemonte, the police were already present. Some agents, disguised as street sweepers, cleared the street of passers-by while watching the entrance to the building where Dozier was imprisoned. Others, equipped with a mechanical shovel, pretended to be workers and blocked access to the street. The NOCS, arriving from Rome, calmly evacuated a supermarket next to the building on Via Pindemonte. They also verified that the door to the BR base was not armoured. The unusual silence in the street quickly alerted the BR. But since the Via Fracchia slaughter, the brigadists had been instructed not to use their weapons in the event of police intervention. They just had to threaten to kill their hostage in order to start a negotiation.[21]

At 11:25 a.m. on 28 January 1982, Major Edoardo Perna and 12 other NOCS men launched the rescue operation. A security team of six men provided cover for Perna and six other agents stormed the flat where five brigadists, including two women, were holding Dozier captive. Perna moved over and overcame one of the women as soon as the door was broken down, which he used as a shield as he ran inside the flat. The brigadist tasked with killing Dozier if a rescue attempt was made was slow to react. As he tried to get inside the tent with a pistol, he was identified and neutralised by one of the NOCS men who ran towards the tent. Dozier, panicked and frightened, fearing the BR would kill him, at first fought with his rescuers. The NOCS assault lasted 50 seconds, without firing a shot.[22] Brigadists Emanuela Frascella, Antonio Savasta, Emilia Libera, Giovanni Ciucci and Cesare Di Lenardo were arrested.

The Dozier case was indicative of the progress that police forces had made since Moro's kidnapping. They used technical means such as wiretapping but also the wealth of information collected in previous years on the radical Left. This work made the success of the NOCS intervention possible. The carabinieri had the GIS formed from the 1st Battalion of Tuscania Airborne Carabinieri.

Carabinieri of the GIS seen during training. (Albert Grandolini collection)

Faced with the disaster caused by Operation Dozier on 18 March 1982, the BR-PCC issued a document announcing a 'strategic retreat'. Understanding that the strategy of attacking the heart of the State led to a deadlock, the organisation, to avoid its disappearance, chose to merge into a working-class victim of the process of industrial restructuring and gave up the offensive in favour of the resistance.[27]

The GIS and the NOCS were made up of selected men who received special military training and had the appropriate technical resources introduced in Italy following the Moro kidnapping. According to journalistic sources, even before Operation Dozier, the NOCS was used in 261 operations resulting in 148 arrests of brigadists, which were carried out without shooting and without loss.[23]

The State's effectiveness was also accompanied by illegal practices such as the use of torture which had been applied sporadically but more methodically in the Dozier case. First, it made it possible to discover the place where the American general was detained, then to obtain the confessions of the five brigadists arrested at Via Pindemonte. According to their accounts, they were taken to a secret apartment and forced to talk under torture. All confessed and spoke to the police except Di Lenardo. At the end of this treatment, which lasted about two days, Libera provided information on eight bases located between Rome and Sardinia, allowing the identification of 22 brigadists. Savasta, who knew perfectly well the reality of the BR in Rome, Veneto and Sardinia, reconstructed the organisation of the columns, causing the arrests of 290 brigadists.[24] The devastation was worse than that caused by Peci's confession.

The failure of Dozier's kidnapping was a huge blow to the BR-PCC. The columns most affected by the arrests were the Venetian column which, in a few weeks, was destroyed and the Roman column which underwent about 40 arrests. The Tuscan Revolutionary Committee, which was on the verge of becoming an operational column, disappeared. The losses were also serious in the Marches, in Sardinia and in Liguria, where some militants tried to reorganise the Genoese column. Some bases were also discovered in Turin and Naples. On 22 April, in Milan, Lo Bianco, of the Genoese column and member of the last BR's CE, was also captured.[25]

In Milan, on 28 February, many members of the Alasia column were arrested. In just three months, the total number of brigadists brought to justice exceeded 200, and more than 20 bases were discovered while many militants took refuge abroad, especially in France, some even in Nicaragua. In the midst of these continuous arrests, on 9 March 1982, Fenzi, imprisoned, dissociated himself from the BR.[26]

The BR-Guerrilla Party

After his break with the CE, Senzani decided to start a 'total social war' and to form a party, the *Brigate Rosse-Partito Guerriglia* (Red Brigades-Guerrilla Party or BR-PG). The new organisation presented itself as a federation of columns and cells, differing substantially from the traditional BR structures accused of elitist drift. On the ideological level, it advocated revolutionary civil war, presented as a vital necessity for the proletariat while NATO and the Warsaw Pact were preparing for a war.[28]

The BR-PG was barely created when they had to face the police forces' blows. On 4 January 1982, Stefano Petrella and Ennio Di Rocco were arrested in Rome while preparing the kidnapping of one of the key men of Italian capitalism, Cesare Romiti.[29] Subjected to torture, they were forced to indicate the houses corresponding to the keys they had in their pockets.[30] After a few days, several brigadists who went to these apartments were arrested, including Giovanni Senzani himself, and also Gino Aldi, Pasquale Giuliano and Susanna Berardi. In the base occupied by Senzani, a real arsenal was found, several surface-to-air missiles, a few bazookas and a mortar that would have been used for the assault on the DC headquarters.[31]

The BR-PG condemned the strategic retreat decision taken in March by the BR-PCC. On 26 April 1982, they even announced the need for a new offensive against the state. A few months earlier, they attacked an armed forces barracks in Salerno and stole two mortars, two rocket launchers, four machine guns, 20 assault rifles and six machine guns. On 12 April, they hit a carabinieri escort in the courtroom of the Foro Italico in Rome then, on 27 April, they killed Raffaele Delcogliano, head of the DC, and his driver Aldo Iermano, in Naples. On 15 July, still in Naples, the head of the mobile police team, Antonio Ammaturo, was killed. During this action, two activists were injured, but managed to escape.[32]

During the summer of 1982, the Italian armed forces became targets for the BR-PG. On 19 August, they organised an assault on the Air Force radio centre on the outskirts of Rome, managing to steal rifles.[33] A week later, on 26 August, in Salerno, a commando of about 15 brigadists ambushed a military convoy, made up of a minibus and a jeep, which travelled between the General Antonio Cascino barracks and the Angelucci barracks. The brigadists blocked the convoy with two cars. A group immobilised and disarmed the occupants of the minibus without eliciting reactions while a second attempted the same action against the jeep, but the

Giovanni Senzani, head of the BR-PG. (Open source)

three corporals who were on board defended themselves and came under gunfire from Nicollo Madau and Antonio Marocco. Corporal Antonio Palumbo, a 22-year-old conscript of the 89th Salerno Infantry Battalion was seriously injured and died of his wounds on 23 September. Hearing the gunshots, a police car arrived at the scene of the ambush. It was immediately hit by bursts of machine gun-fire from Russo which wounded passers-by, Salvatore De Sio, 19, and Lorena Trevisone, seven. At that moment, Marcello Ghiringhelli intervened and killed the agent sitting behind the wheel, Antonio Bandiera, while two other agents fled and the last one, Mario De Marco, tried to react before being seriously injured; he died on 30 August. While until then, the BR had always avoided 'civilians' being affected during their operations, two passers-by, including a little girl, were wounded in Salerno, demonstrating the operational weakness of the BR-PG.[34]

This impression was reinforced when, on 21 October, in Turin, during a robbery at the Banco di Napoli, the BR-PG coldly executed two security guards, unarmed and taken hostage, with two bullets to the head. The gratuitousness of this cruel act shocked the population and tended to isolate the BR-PG even more. It was in these circumstances that Franceschini, who was nevertheless favourable to the BR-PG, declared his leaving the BR and abandoning the armed struggle, causing a rupture in what remained of the historical nucleus. Curcio, meanwhile, began to reflect on the results of the armed struggle with a collective of prisoners and admitted that the cycle of struggles that began in the 1970s was over.[35]

After the theft at the Banco di Napoli, and beyond the shock caused to the militants by the madness of this action, the BR-PG was quickly decimated by arrests. In October 1982, Vittorio Bolognesi and 10 other militants were arrested in Naples, resulting in the fall of five bases. These arrests triggered a chain reaction of denunciation and repentance which led to the arrest of Nadia Ligas and Antonio Chiocchi, one of the leaders of the Neapolitan column, but also of various leaders of the BR-PCC in Turin and members of Alasia column.[36]

If the end of 1982 was fatal for the BR-PG, it was also so for the Alasia column. In a robbery in Lissone, in the province of Milan, on 16 July 1982, where a carabiniere was killed, it lost an activist, Stefano Ferrari, who was fatally injured. On the 23rd, Mario Protti and Vincenzo Scaccia fell into the hands of the police. In November, following the revelations of Marocco, the police discovered the last base of the Alasia column in Cinisello.[37] The survivors of the column found refuge in Cremona in a house made available to them by a sympathiser. But on 31 January 1983, the police broke into this base and arrested five activists.[38] This was the end for the Walter Alasia column.

The BR-PCCs in the European Anti-imperialist Struggle

The repression also hit the BR-PCC hard. On 26 April 1982, Umberto Catabiani, member of the DS, was killed.[39] Marcello Capuano, one of the main leaders of the Roman column, was captured in the capital on 30 March after being seriously injured.[40] However, at the start of 1983, the BR-PCC organisation was the last BR formation still active.

Under the leadership of Barbara Balzerani, the BR-PCC tried to concentrate its forces on the labour world disrupted by the agreement on the salary scale signed between the employers and the unions on 22 January 1983. This agreement, which allowed massive layoffs and a cut in social spending, led to strikes and demonstrations. The BR-PCC wanted to join the fight against the agreement and on 3 May 1983 in Rome, injured Gino Giugni; a university professor and member of the PSI Central Committee and one of the architects of the January agreement.[41] Nonetheless, it did not make the news for the rest of 1983.

It was not until 15 February 1984 that the BR-PCC, in coordination with the Lebanese Revolutionary Armed Faction, struck again by killing, in Rome, Leamon Hunt, Director General of the Multinational Force and Observers in the Sinai. This action was part of the logic of the attack against American imperialism which, along with the social question, constituted the second front of the BR-PCC. According to the organisation, the multinational force only served to guarantee the safeguarding of American interests in the Middle East against the Palestinians. The attack on Hunt was therefore an act of war against imperialism.[42] It did not prevent, however, the division from settling within the BR-PCC.

In the spring of 1984, for the majority of the members of the BR-PCC, the armed struggle remained decisive and merged with revolutionary policy in the context of a protracted people's war. This faction, nicknamed 1st position, was opposed to a minority, which took the name of 2nd position. The latter wanted to get out of the logic of armed confrontation and identified new forms of political action in which military operation should be discreet and local. The open discussion within the BR-PCC between these two factions took place mainly in France, where a large number of militants had taken refuge. In the second half of 1984, the militants of the 2nd position were finally expelled from the BR-PCC.

The 1st position militants, who kept the name of BR-PCC, remained faithful to the idea that a revolutionary minority would eventually become the majority through daily political work accompanied by military actions. Despite this loyalty to the military tradition of the old BR, the BR-PCCs had weak operational capacities. During an attempted robbery, on 14 December 1984, they attacked an armoured van, but the group's lack of preparation led to the failure of the operation which ended with the death of an activist, Antonio Gustini, and the capture of Cecilia Massara.[43]

Barbara Balzerani, seen after her arrest in June 1985. (Open source)

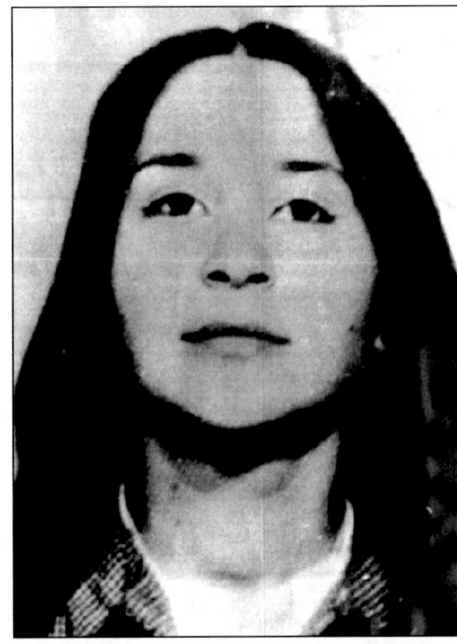

Wilma Monaco, shown on her ID-photo. (Polizia di Stato)

Despite these setbacks, on 27 March 1985 in Rome, Ezio Tarantelli, professor of political economy at the Sapienza University as well as president of the CISL Institute for Labour Studies and Economics, was shot dead by the BR-PCC with a Skorpion submachine gun in the university car park. This attack was linked to the referendum about abrogation of the indexation of wages on inflation. Tarantelli, convinced of the need to reform the labour market, was strongly committed to the repeal.[44] The referendum took place and its result marked a new defeat for the workers' movement.

Meanwhile, the Special Anticrime Section in Rome was continuing its investigations. On 13 December 1984, the French police, during a major anti-terrorist operation, arrested some members of *Action Directe* in Paris and several members of the BR living in the French capital for several months.[45] After Tarantelli's death, carabinieri arrested several members of the BR-PCC including Maura Di Gioia and Vittorio Antonini. In June 1985, they arrested Barbara Balzerani, who was still working to unify the organisation and restore political momentum to the armed struggle. The investigations that led to her arrest began the previous October. After identifying Wilma Monaco, carabinieri found the trail of her husband, Gianni Pelosi, expatriate in France since 1976. After surveillance, Pelosi was finally spotted in Rome and arrested with Balzerani.[46]

In the autumn, 2nd position BR-PCC activists, led by Geraldina Colotti, Paolo Cassetta and Wilma Monaco, returned from France to organise a new formation in Rome, the *Brigate Rosse-Unione dei Comunisti Combattenti* (Red Brigades-Union of Combatant Communists or BR-UCC) whose objective was to transform partial struggles into general struggles leading to the overthrow of the capitalist order.[47] The BR-UCC was recruiting young activists between Rome and Bologna, where investigations were also carried out to identify possible targets. The choice fell on Antonio Da Empoli, director of the Department of Economic and Social Affairs of Prime Minister Bettino Craxi. The BR-UCC took action on 26 February 1986. But the Da Empoli investigation was conducted superficially and no one knew that the economist's driver was in fact a policeman. At the time of the attack, the latter reacted by killing Wilma Monaco.[48]

After almost a year of silence, the BR-PCC struck again on 10 February 1986, killing Lando Conti, former mayor of Florence.[49] According to the perpetrators of the attack, the man collaborated in greater Italian integration into NATO and in the Star Wars military project, promoted by Reagan's US administration, through the Italian Consortium for Strategic Technologies. After Conti's murder, the BR-PCC temporarily stopped conducting actions and it was not until 14 February 1987 that the organisation launched an attack on a postal van. The ambush took place at 8:45 a.m., on Via dei Prati dei Papa, a narrow street in Rome. The postal van was blocked by the brigadists while the police car following the van, having no clear

Firearms and other materiel captured at the BR-PCC base in Rome, in 1987. (Albert Grandolini collection)

view, hit it. The three policemen in the car did not have time to react before they were hit by bullets from pistols, submachine guns and hunting rifles. Officers Rolando Lanari and Giuseppe Scravaglieri died in the shooting, while Pasquale Parente was seriously injured. The commando stole a large sum of money and fled while firing machine guns at the surrounding buildings to intimidate the inhabitants and prevent them from seeing the direction taken by their two cars.[50]

The ambush on Via dei Prati dei Papa, because of its brutality now foreign to social conflicts, aroused great emotion in the population who feared that the country would fall back into the violence of the 1970s. Carabinieri had long been investigating the BR-PCC and BR-UCC. Shortly before, after a shooting on 22 January 1987, they captured Paolo Cassetta, Fabrizio Melorio and Geraldina Colotti, members of the BR-UCC.[51]

The BR's End

The arrests and the political isolation of the BR-UCC were leading to an end. They carried out their last action on 20 March 1987 by killing Air Force General Licio Giorgieri, director since 1983 of the aeronautical and space weapons and armaments construction section. If, on 24 March during the Moro trial, Gallinari claimed responsibility for the murder of the General, other brigadists such as Semeria, Azzolini and Cecco Bellosi condemned it.[52]

Collaboration between the various European police forces was strengthening and led to a series of arrests. In April 1987, the Spanish police dismantled the BR-UCC group based in Barcelona, while in June, Maurizio Locusta was arrested in Paris. In June, the DS was captured in Rome while two important bases were discovered. The BR-UCC then ceased to exist as an operational organisation and its militants, who remained at large, dispersed. The BR-PCC remained the last offspring of the armed struggle, still active even though it took almost a year before they carried out their last murderous action.

It was in this climate of confusion that in February 1987, in the Rome court bunker, the authorities seized a document on Nadia Ponti, which was later published in certain newspapers. It was a declaration signed by Curcio, Moretti, Iannelli and Bertolazzi in which they declared the experience of armed struggle over.[53] Barbara Balzerani signed the document in the autumn with seven other brigadists. This document was nevertheless rejected by other prisoners such as Piccioni, Seghetti, Lo Bianco or Gallinari. The latter even organised an attempt to break out of Rebibbia prison in order to resume the fight and unify what remained of the BR forces. But the escape plan was discovered in April by the guards.[54]

On 16 April 1988 in Forli, the BR-PCC committed their last action. Brigadists Stefano Minguzzi and Franco Grilli, dressed as postmen, rang the home doorbell of Roberto Ruffilli, expert in institutional problems, collaborator of the Prime Minister and DC secretary. They entered the house, led Ruffilli to his living room, made him kneel and shot him in the back of the neck.[55] This action was part of an anti-imperialist armed struggle on a European scale in a strategic alliance with the RAF and *Action Directe*. The text of the RAF and the BR-PCC joint statement called on the fighting forces of Western Europe to unify.[56] Despite these internationalist proclamations, the BR-PCC was in agony. In the first days of September 1988 a vast carabineri operation, carried out in the regions of Lazio and Tuscany, led to practically all the members of the organisation who remained in Italy being imprisoned. Finally, it was in Paris in September 1989 that the BR-PCC DS base was discovered. French police arrested activists as carabinieri captured Carla Vendetti, one of the organisation's leaders, arriving from Paris.[57]

With the arrests of 1988, the BR no longer existed as an organisation on Italian soil. This was also the time when the main leaders in prison wrote convergent texts on the problem of ending the armed struggle. On 23 October 1988, Gallinari, Abatangelo, Cassetta, Lo Bianco, Locusta, Pancelli, Piccioni and Seghetti sent a document to the press in which they declared that the war against the state was over, and the defeat of the revolutionary movement was recognised.[58] The history of the BR ended while that of the ex-brigadists began.

At the end of the 1980s, the brigadists were either in prison, in exile abroad, or free in Italy since their involvement in the BR was not known to the authorities. The most numerous were the prisoners. Their statutes were diverse. Some had chosen to become repenters, meaning that they collaborated with the authorities in exchange for reduced prison sentences. This was the case for the most famous, Patricio Peci, and also for Savasta, Emilia Libera and Massimo Cianfanelli. The majority of prisoners chose the status of dissociated. They undertook to recognise all the crimes with which they were accused and to renounce the use of violence as a means of political struggle. The other prisoners, neither repented nor dissociated, formed the cohort of diehards, the best known of which were Moretti and Balzerani.

Many fugitive militants emigrated, most of them to France, where they were able, thanks to the 'Mitterrand doctrine', to start a

From left to right: Fiori, Gallinari, and Moretti, seen during their trial, in 1983. (Albert Grandolini collection)

By the early 1980s, even the PCI began calling for an end to BR's terrorism – as show in graffiti such as this. (Albert Grandolini collection)

new life. Faced with severe Italian anti-terrorism legislation in 1985, the French president verbally promised that the fugitives who had taken refuge in France would not be extradited if they renounced the armed struggle.[59] In the mid-1980s, around 300 Italian far-left activists enjoyed French hospitality, despite criticism from Italian authorities.[60] Since then, Rome has not stopped asking Paris for the extradition of the former brigadists. In this context, the arrests on 28 April 2021 of ex-BR Roberta Cappelli, Giovani Alimonti, Enzo Calvitti, Marina Petrella and Sergio Tornaghi on the orders of President Emmanuel Macron were welcomed by the Italian government.[61]

Some had not chosen France as a refuge. Casimirri settled in Nicaragua where he still enjoyed the protection of the Sandinistas. Lojacono took refuge in Switzerland, of which he had nationality through his mother. Rita Algranati followed Casimirri to Nicaragua before settling in Angola and then in Algeria. She was finally arrested in Cairo in January 2004 and extradited to Italy.

Rarer were the former brigadists who had never been discovered or whose actions were underestimated. Thus Raimondo Etro, who participated in the preparations for Moro's kidnapping, was only sentenced to one year in prison in 1985. But in 1994 his involvement in the Via Fani ambush was discovered. He was sentenced to 20 years in prison and released in 2010. Germano Maccari was not exposed until 1993. He was sentenced to 30 years in prison, where he died in 2001.

The BR's struggle and more broadly that of the armed Left organisations was still the subject of unanimous condemnation in Italy, as shown by the sentence of life imprisonment in 2019 to Cesare Battisti, former member of the group Armed Proletarians for Communism. While it was understandable that the families of victims of the armed struggle were asking for justice and reparation, the state's attitude nevertheless appeared extremely severe, especially when compared with the fate of neo-fascist terrorists. None of the perpetrators of the Piazza Fontana bombing was convicted. It should be remembered that the BR had never committed an attack on the wider population. This did not mean that the far-left had the right to kill, but that their targets had always been individualised with a political character. There was also no doubt that the BR militants were wrong, not only in their methods, but in their analysis of the balance of power and changes in society. They paid dearly for it.

The Italian State's intransigence vis-à-vis the BR lasts until this day. Was there a way to forget the support they received from part of the population, at least until the Moro kidnapping? Was this support not a reaction to another violence, that of the state first but above all that, silent and bloodless, of a social and economic system whose survival always required austerity, unemployment, job insecurity, not to mention attacks against nature? Was it not the resurgence of that political and social violence that ran through the history of contemporary Italy, far removed from the tourist clichés of la dolce vita? This violence was expressed in the political world which allowed fascism to gain power in 1922 or led to the severity in the DC repression in response to the aspirations of the people in 1968, while the European countries engaged in a policy of consensus, then of reforms. In this sense, the apology for violence by some leftist groups was already well anchored in the culture of the country. Rather than trying to understand, not absolve, the BR's struggle in the light of this violence, is it not easier to want to demonstrate that they were being manipulated by the KGB, the CIA or other mysterious organisations?

CONCLUSION

If there was a mystery in the BR's history, it was above all that of their longevity and their significant operational capacity. In its first years of existence, the organisation set rather modest objectives since it defined itself as the tool with which the proletariat would go from a violent but spontaneous response, like that of the 1969 Hot Autumn to an organised attack on capitalism. This phase of the BR's existence was the least violent and had different characteristics. The organisation was only present in the north of the country, mainly in Milan and then Turin, it acted mainly in the factories and attracted the sympathy of a fringe of the working class. It was not very different then from the French *Gauche prolétarienne* even if it did not have the same media success.

The years 1974 to 1975 marked the first turning point for the BR who gradually abandoned the armed propaganda strategy in favour of confrontation with the state. The BR then extended their zone of action towards Genoa, Veneto and above all Rome, which was not an industrial centre but the heart of the Italian State. The radicalisation and militarisation of the organisation then lead to a headlong rush that was conducive to the BR becoming a central phenomenon in Italian history and, during the Moro kidnapping, a crucial element.

From Moro's death, the BR degenerated, lost contact with the working class, and became locked into a struggle against the state that was both sterile and nihilistic. The latter ultimately won the war declared against it, but for this it was forced to use all the repressive potential at its disposal, imposing special laws and suspending certain constitutional guarantees. The harshness of the repression, the severity of the sentences and the absence of amnesty signalled a certain vision of civil society considered hostile because it offered asylum and protection to the internal enemy and had to be eliminated forever.

The crushing of the BR was also accompanied by an enterprise of delegitimisation. To the Right, the BR had been nothing more than puppets of international terrorism headed by Moscow, an interpretation that was part of the Cold War tradition still prevalent in contemporary Italy. More surprisingly, the Left had taken up the same theme, just changing the identity of the sponsors which it considered to be Washington, the Italian secret service or NATO's secret networks. Manipulated from the outside, the BR would therefore have no connection with Italian social and political reality, nor rooted in the country's working-class tradition. They were thus thrown into a historical beyond, like monstrous chimeras or bad dreams populated by occult machinations.

This is to forget that the BR are part of a singular history, that of the Italian working class in a country where the state has always been weak and lacked popular support. This working class has always leaned towards radicalism, it made the PCI the most powerful party in Western Europe, it placed in it its dreams of social changes, it believed at the time of the Liberation War of 1944–1945 that the revolution was near, after its moderation had not blunted its revolutionary aspirations. The men and women who embarked on the BR adventure believed in this revolutionary myth and wanted to revive it when they were convinced that the PCI had abandoned it.

It was the power of this myth that made the BR's strength. It was so rooted in the Italian Left that despite the arrests, new brigadists joined the organisation for more than 10 years. It explains the importance of the network of sympathisers without whom the BR would have been unable to survive and shake the country. To this must be added, of course, the structures that the BR had given themselves, at the same time flexible, mobile and compartmentalised to give the least control to the blows of the police forces.

The trajectory of the BR condensed in a few years the myths of the Italian Left in the twentieth century, those of the proletarian revolution, the assault on the Winter Palace, the partisans' struggles in the context of the political and social polarisation that marked the end of the 1960s. But it occurred in a phase of deep transformation of the capitalist system which saw the transition from the Italian miracle economy with its Fordist factories and large workforce to a world where the worker was the victim of the automation, robotisation in a context of deindustrialisation. The time had passed for revolution, or even for the welfare state at the end of the 1970s. The brigadist dream of urban guerrilla warfare was incomprehensible at a time when trench warfare prevailed to confront economic liberalisation. The failure of the BR heralded the twilight of communism and the revolutionary dream.

SELECTED BIBLIOGRAPHY

Primary Sources

Adriano, Pino, *Une mort de plomb. Qui a tué Mauro Brutto?* (Librairie Vuibert, 2016)

Agosti, Aldo, *Palmiro Togliatti* (IB Tauris, 2008)

Armeni, Gianremo, *La strategia vincente del generale Dalla Chiesa contro le Brigate Rosse… e la mafia* (Edizione Associate, 2004)

Balestrini, Nanni & Moroni, Primo, *La horde d'or. La grande vague révolutionnaire et créative, politique et existentielle. Italie, 1968-1977* (L'éclat, 2017; édition italienne, 1988)

Balzerani, Barbara, *Camarade Lune* (Cambourakis, 2017)

Bartali, Roberto, 'Il PCI e le Brigate Rosse', in Sechi, Salvatore, Le vene aperte del delitto Moro. Terrorismo, PCI, trame et servizi segreti (Polistampa, 2009), p.92

Bartali, Roberto et al., 'Infiltrati nelle Brigate rosse', in Il sequestro di verità. I buchi neri del delitto Moro (Kaos Edizioni, 2008), p.20

Bianco, Romano & Castronuovo, Manlio, *Via Fani ore 9.02* (Nutrimenti, 2010)

Clementi, Marco, *Storia delle Brigate Rosse* (Odradek, 2007)

Colarizi, Simona, *Storia politica della repubblica 1943-2006* (Laterza, 2007)

Colarizi, Simona, 'Un'introduzione agli anni dell'inquietudine', in Marc Lazar, Marie-Anne Matard-Bonucci, Il libro degli anni di piombo (Rizzoli, 2010), p.138

Di Petrillo, Domenico, *Il lungo assedio. La lotta al terrorismo nel diario operativo della Sezione Speciale Anticrimine Carabinieri di Roma* (Melampo, 2018)

Falanga, Gianluca, *Spie dall'est. L'Italia nelle carte segrete della Stasi* (Carocci, 2014)

Fenzi, Enrico, *Armes et bagages. Journal des Brigades Rouges* (Les Belles Lettres, 2008; édition italienne, 2006)

Foro, Philippe, *Une longue saison de douleur et de mort. L'affaire Aldo Moro* (Vendémiaire, 2011)

Franceschini, Alberto, *Brigades rouges. L'histoire secrète des BR racontée par leur fondateur* (Panama, 2005)

Galli, Giorgio, *Piombo rosso. La storia completa della lotta armata in Italia dal 1970 a oggi* (Baldini & Castoldi, 2013)

Gallinari, Prospero, *Un contadino nella metropoli* (Bompiani, 2006)

Guigou, Jacques & Wajnsztejn, Jacques, *Mai 68 et le Mai rampant italien* (L'Harmattan, Paris, 2008)

Jansen, Christian, 'Brigate Rosse und Rote Armee Fraktion. ProtagonistInnen, Propaganda und Praxis des Terrorismus der frühen siebziger Jahre', in Oliver von Mengersen et al., Personen – Soziale Bewegungen – Parteien. Beiträge zur Neuesten Geschichte. Festschrift für Hartmut Soell (Manutius, 2004), p.491

Marini Recchia, Vincenzo & Zupo, Giuseppe, *Operazione Moro* (Franco Angeli Editore, 1984)

Moran, Sue Ellen (ed.), *Court Depositions of Three Red Brigadists* (DTIC, February 1986)

Moretti, Mario, *Brigate Rosse. Une histoire italienne* (Editions Amsterdam, 2010; édition italienne 1998)

Oliva, Gianni, *Anni di piombo e di tritolo. 1969-1980, il terrorismo nero et il terrorismo rosso da piazza Fontana alla strage di Bologna* (Mondadori, 2019)

Orlandi, Fernando, 'A Praga, a Praga!' in Sechi, Salvatore, Le vene aperte del delitto Moro (Polistampa, 2009), pp.119–161

Orsini, Alessandro *Anatomia delle Brigate Rosse* (Rubbettino, 2010)

Padovani, Marcelle, *Vivre avec le terrorisme. Le modèle italien* (Calmann-Lévy, 1982)

Santalena, Elisa, 'La figure controversée de Mario Moretti, entre histoire et suspicion', colloque *Littérature et "temps de révoltes", (Italie 1967-1980)'* (November 2008), <http://colloque-temps-revoltes.ens-lyon.fr/spip.php?article74#acte>

Sommier, Isabelle, *La violence politique et son deuil. L'après 68 en France et en Italie* (Presses universitaires de Rennes, 1998)

US Senate, 'Terrorism and Security: The Italian Experience', *Report of the Subcommittee on Security and Terrorism of the Committee on the Judiciary United States Senate* (November 1984)

Wievorka, Michel, *Sociétés et terrorisme* (Fayard, 1988)

Secondary Sources

Bruni, Marco, *Il caso Moro negli atti del Ministero per la sicurezza di Stato della Repubblica Democratica Tedesca* (Sapienza Università di Roma, 2015)

Buckingham, Larry Allen, *The Red Brigades: A description of a Terrorist Organization* (California State University, 1982)

DeGhetto, Todd H., *Precipitating the Decline of Terrorist Groups: A Systems Analysis* (Naval Postgraduate School, 1994)

Dogliotti, Chiara, *Le colonne e la città. Le cellule brigatiste e il loro rapporto con il territorio, 1969-1982. I casi di Genova, di Napoli e del Veneto* (Università di Pisa, 2016-2017)

Guidon, Guillaume, *Images de la violence, violence des images. La violence politique et sa représentation dans la photographie de presse italienne (1969-1984)* (Université de Grenoble-Alpes, 2010)

Guzzo, Domenico, *Rome, l'inscription des violences politiques dans la ville au cours des années de plombs: (1966-1982)* (Université Grenoble-Alpes, 2017)

Stortoni, Luciana, *La repressione del terrorismo in Italia: l'intervento delle forze dell'ordine fina all'inizio degli anni ottanta* (Istitutio Universitario Europeo, 1992)

Articles

Falciola, Luca, 'Transnational Relationships between the Italian Revolutionary Left and Palestinian Militants during the Cold War' in *Journal of Cold War Studies*, 22:4 (Fall 2020), pp.31–70

Joahny, Stéphane, 'Quand Paris servait de base arrière aux Brigades rouges', *Le Journal du dimanche* (14 July 2018)

Orlandi, Fernando, 'La prima volta del KGB sulle Brigate rosse', in *East Europe and Asia Strategies*, 34 (February 2011), pp.25–26

Pesta, Mikulas, 'The Origins of the Left-wing Terrorism after 1968', *Dvacáté století – The Twentieth Century* (2014/1), p.68

Ploetz, Michael, 'Mit RAF, Roten Brigaden und Action Directe Terrorismus und Rechtsextremismus in der Strategie von SED und KPdSU', *Zeitschrift des Forschungsverbundes SED-Staat*, 22 (2007), pp.134–135

Quirico, Stefano, 'Il modello organizzativo delle Brigate rosse in una prospettiva comparata', *Quaderno di storia contemporanea*, 31:44 (2008), pp.61–88

Richelson, Jeffrey T., 'Truth Conquers All Chains: The U.S. Army Intelligence Support Activity, 1981-1989', *International Journal of Intelligence and CounterIntelligence*, 12:2 (1999), pp.168–200

Steenbeek, Ralf, 'De bestrijding van de Rode Brigades in Italië, 1974-1975. De methode van generaal Carlo Alberto Dalla Chiesa', *Leidschrift*, 23:1 (April 2008), p.117

Much information can be consulted on various websites and online archives. The reports and hearings of the numerous parliamentary inquiry committees are available on various websites, for example parlamento.it or gerograssi.it. Many BR texts are available on bibliotecamarxista.org. We must also cite various websites such as ugomariatassinari.it, insorgenze.net, and archivio900.it.

NOTES

Introduction

1 Michel Wievorka, *Sociétés et terrorisme* (Fayard, 1988), p.145.
2 We do not use the term myth without its common meaning, that of lies, but in that by Georges Sorel: a mental representation that allows the people to mobilise, to fight, to transform.

Chapter 1

1 Aldo Agosti, *Palmiro Togliatti* (IB Tauris, 2008), pp.151–152.
2 Isabelle Sommier, *La violence politique et son deuil. L'après 68 en France et en Italie* (Presses universitaires de Rennes, 1998), p.155.
3 Gianni Oliva, *Anni di piombo e di tritolo. 1969-1980, il terrorismo nero et il terrorismo rosso da piazza Fontana alla strage di Bologna*, (Mondadori, 2019), p.85.
4 Pino Adriano, *Une mort de plomb. Qui a tué Mauro Brutto?* (Vuibert, 2016), p.122.
5 Aldo Agosti, p.194.
6 Simona Colarizi, *Storia politica della repubblica 1943-2006* (Laterza, 2007), pp.39–46.
7 SIFAR became *Servizio Informazioni Difesa* (Defence Information Service or SID) in 1965. It reported to the Ministry of Defence.
8 Gianni Oliva, pp.86–87.
9 Gianni Oliva, p.110.
10 Alberto Franceschini, *Brigades rouges. L'histoire secrète des BR racontée par leur fondateur* (Panama, 2005), p.47. Franceschini, then 13 years old, witnessed the clashes in Reggio Emilia, his hometown.
11 Gianni Oliva, p.112.
12 Nanni Balestrini & Primo Moroni, *La horde d'or. Italie 1968-1977* (L'éclat, 2017), pp.38–39.
13 Gianni Oliva, p.113.
14 Luciana Stortoni, *La repressione del terrorismo in Italia: l'intervento delle forze dell'ordine fina all'inizio degli anni ottanta* (Istitutio Universitario Europeo, 1992), p.269.
15 Gianni Oliva, p.118.
16 http://www.bibliotecamarxista.org/mafai/cap%204.htm
17 Jacques Guigou & Jacques Wajnsztejn, *Mai 68 et le Mai rampant italien* (L'Harmattan, Paris, 2008).
18 Giorgio Galli, *Piombo rosso. La storia completa della lotta armata in Italia dal 1970 a oggi* (Baldini & Castoldi, 2013), p.8.
19 Isabelle Sommier, *La violence politique et son deuil*, p.174.
20 Isabelle Sommier, *La violence politique et son deuil*, p.160.
21 Gianni Oliva, pp.106–108.
22 Philippe Foro, *Une longue saison de douleur et de mort* (Vendémiaire, 2011), p.15.
23 Simona Colarizi, 'Un'introduzione agli anni dell'inquietudine', in Marc Lazar, Marie-Anne Matard-Bonucci, Il libro degli anni di piombo (Rizzoli, 2010), p.138.
24 There were violent protests outside the US Consulate in Florence on 23 April 1967 and during Richard Nixon's visit to Rome on 2 March 1969.
25 Philippe Foro, p.16.
26 Gianni Oliva, p.121.
27 Michel Wievorka, p.190.
28 Gianni Oliva, p.123.
29 Domenico Guzzo, *Rome, l'inscription des violences politique dans la ville au cours des années de plombs (1966-1982)* (Université Grenoble-Alpes, 2017), pp.412–417.
30 Nanni Balestrini & Primo Moroni, pp.244–246.
31 Gianni Oliva, p.131.
32 Gianni Oliva, pp.134–135.
33 Nanni Balestrini & Primo Moroni, p.313.
34 Mario Moretti, *Brigate Rosse. Une histoire italienne* (Editions Amsterdam, 2010) (édition italienne 1998), p.52.
35 Nanni Balestrini & Primo Moroni, p.366.
36 Nanni Balestrini & Primo Moroni, p.313.
37 Commissione parlamentare d'inchiesta sulla strage di via Fani, sul sequestro e l'assassinio di Aldo Moro e sul terrorismo in Italia, Doc XXIII, n. 5, Vol. 4, 1984, p.58.

Chapter 2

1 Mikulas Pesta, 'The Origins of the Left-wing Terrorism after 1968', *Dvacáté století - The Twentieth Century*, (2014/1), p.68.
2 http://www.bibliotecamarxista.org/soccorso%20rosso/capitolo%201.htm
3 Gianni Oliva, p.142.
4 Gianni Oliva, p.141.
5 Giorgio Galli, p.19.
6 Isabelle Sommier, *La violence politique et son deuil*, p.79.
7 Marcelle Padovani, *Vivre avec le terrorisme. Le modèle italien* (Calmann-Levy, 1982), pp.109–111.
8 Marco Clementi, *Storia delle Brigate Rosse* (Odradek, 2007), p.48.
9 Mikulas Pesta, p.68.
10 Mikulas Pesta, p.63.
11 Marco Clementi, p.11.
12 Mario Moretti, p.62.
13 Prospero Gallinari, *Un contadino nella metropoli* (Bompiani, 2006), p.57.
14 Alberto Franceschini, pp.65–77
15 Nanni Balestrini & Primo Moroni, p.382.
16 Gianni Oliva, pp.15–22.
17 Nanni Balestrini & Primo Moroni, pp.320–321.
18 Marco Clementi, p.17
19 Gianni Oliva, p.150.
20 Nanni Balestrini & Primo Moroni, p.384.
21 Giorgio Galli, p.11.
22 Gianni Oliva, p.151.
23 Gianni Oliva, p.25.
24 Mario Moretti, p.63.
25 Commissione parlamentare d'inchiesta sulla strage di via Fani, sul sequestro e l'assassinio di Aldo Moro e sul terrorismo in Italia, Doc XXIII, n. 5, Vol. 4, 1984, p.62.
26 Giorgio Galli, p.10.
27 Mario Moretti, p.35.
28 Prospero Gallinari, p.72.
29 Prospero Gallinari, p.74.
30 Gianni Oliva, p.158.
31 Mario Moretti, p.55.
32 Mikulas Pesta, pp.69–70.
33 Marco Clementi, p.19.
34 Giorgio Galli, p.12.
35 Chiara Dogliotti, *Le colonne e la città. Le cellule brigatiste e il loro rapporto con il territorio, 1969-1982. I casi di Genova, di Napoli e del Veneto* (Università di Pisa, 2016-2017), p.59.
36 Mikulas Pesta, p.68.
37 Marco Clementi, p.41.
38 Alberto Franceschini, p.155.
39 Nanni Balestrini & Primo Moroni, p.385.
40 Giorgio Galli, p.14.
41 Gianni Oliva, p.151.

Chapter 3

1 Michel Wievorka, p.150.
2 Stefano Quirico, 'Il modello organizzativo delle Brigate rosse in una prospettiva comparata', in *Quaderno di storia contemporanea*, 31:44 (2008), p.63.
3 Marco Clementi, p.36.
4 Giorgio Galli, p.21.
5 Nanni Balestrini & Primo Moroni, p.367.
6 http://www.bibliotecamarxista.org/soccorso%20rosso/capitolo%205.htm

7 Giorgio Galli, p.16.
8 Mario Moretti, pp.70–71.
9 Gianni Oliva, p.159.
10 Commissione parlamentare d'inchiesta sulla strage di via Fani, sul sequestro e l'assassinio di Aldo Moro e sul terrorismo in Italia, Doc XXIII, n. 5, Vol. 4, 1984, p.59.
11 Marco Clementi, p.25.
12 Alberto Franceschini, p.141.
13 Marco Clementi, p.34.
14 Mario Moretti, p.73.
15 Marco Clementi, pp.27–28.
16 Mikulas Pesta, p.69.
17 Marco Clementi, p.33.
18 Marco Clementi, pp.37–38.
19 Elisa Santalena, 'La figure controversée de Mario Moretti, entre histoire et suspicion', colloque *Littérature et "temps de révoltes", (Italie 1967-1980)*, <http://colloque-temps-revoltes.ens-lyon.fr/spip.php?article74#acte>
20 Nanni Balestrini & Primo Moroni p.392.
21 Mario Moretti, p.76.
22 Giorgio Galli, p.24.
23 Marco Clementi, p.39.
24 Marco Clementi, p.40.
25 Commissione parlamentare d'inchiesta sul terrorismo in Italia e sulle cause della mancata individuazione dei responsabili delle stragi, Doc XXIII, n. 64, volume primo, Tomo 6, 2001, p.6.
26 Roberto Bartali et al., 'Infiltrati nelle Brigate rosse', in Il sequestro di verità. I buchi neri del delitto Moro (Kaos Edizioni, 2008), p.20.
27 Commissione parlamentare d'inchiesta sulla strage di via Fani, sul sequestro e l'assassinio di Aldo Moro e sul terrorismo in Italia, Doc XXIII, n. 5, Vol. 1, 1983, p.56.
28 Mario Moretti, p.77.
29 Mario Moretti, p.104.
30 Giorgio Galli, pp.31–32.
31 Marco Clementi, p.51.
32 Mario Moretti, pp.110–111.
33 Marco Clementi, p.51.
34 Marco Clementi, p.52.
35 Mario Moretti, pp.105–107.
36 Giorgio Galli, p.39.
37 Gianni Oliva, p.161.
38 Gianni Oliva, p.162.
39 Alberto Franceschini, p.203.
40 Gianni Oliva, p.163.
41 Marco Clementi, p.57.
42 http://www.bibliotecamarxista.org/soccorso%20rosso/capitolo%2013.htm
43 Giorgio Galli, pp.41–42.
44 Isabelle Sommier, p.168.
45 Gianni Oliva, p.192.
46 Gianni Oliva, p.164.
47 http://www.bibliotecamarxista.org/soccorso%20rosso/capitolo%2014.htm
48 Giorgio Galli, p.46.
49 Chiara Dogliotti, *Le colonne e la città. Le cellule brigatiste e il loro rapporto con il territorio, 1969-1982. I casi di Genova, di Napoli e del Veneto* (Università di Pisa, 2016-2017), pp.184–187.
50 Chiara Dogliotti, *Le colonne e la città. Le cellule brigatiste e il loro rapporto con il territorio, 1969-1982. I casi di Genova, di Napoli e del Veneto* (Università di Pisa, 2016-2017), p.25.

Chapter 4

1 Marco Clementi, p.64.
2 Chiara Dogliotti, p.69.
3 Commissione parlamentare di inchiesta sul rapimento e sulla morte di Aldo Moro, Doc 23, N. 29, 2017, p.16.
4 https://www.ugomariatassinari.it/alfredo-buonavita/
5 Chiara Dogliotti, p.69.
6 Mario Moretti, p.122.
7 Gianni Oliva, p.168.
8 Todd H. DeGhetto, *Precipitating the Decline of Terrorist Groups: A Systems Analysis* (Naval Postgraduate School, 1994), p.55.
9 Commissione parlamentare d'inchiesta sul terrorismo in Italia e sulle cause della mancata individuazione dei responsabili delle stragi, Doc XXIII, n. 64, volume primo, Tomo 6, 2001, p.162.
10 Alberto Franceschini, pp.225–230.
11 Marco Clementi, p.70.
12 Giorgio Galli, p.53.
13 Chiara Dogliotti, p.71.
14 Marco Clementi, p.75.
15 Gianni Oliva, p.170.
16 Giorgio Galli, pp.54–55.
17 Alberto Franceschini, p.234.
18 Giorgio Galli, p.56.
19 Gianni Oliva, p.172.
20 http://www.bibliotecamarxista.org/soccorso%20rosso/capitolo%2015.htm
21 Giorgio Galli, p.61.
22 Prospero Gallinari, p.93.
23 Giorgio Galli, p.61.
24 Chiara Dogliotti, pp.191–192.
25 Gianni Oliva, p.174.
26 Marco Clementi, p.99.
27 Gianni Oliva, pp.194–196.
28 Gianni Oliva, p.201.
29 Mario Moretti, p.127.
30 Alberto Franceschini, p.277.
31 Gianni Oliva, pp.143–144.
32 Marco Clementi, p.102.
33 Commissione parlamentare d'inchiesta sul terrorismo in Italia e sulle cause della mancata individuazione dei responsabili delle stragi (Cs), XIII Legislatura, elenco audizioni, 73a seduta, 5 juli 2000.
34 Relazione della Commissione parlamentare d'inchiesta sulla strage di via Fani, sul sequestro e l'assassinio di Aldo Moro e sul terrorismo in Italia (Rome 1983), vol. 4, Carlo Alberto Dalla Chiesa, 8 juli 1980, p.290.
35 Gianni Oliva, p.175.
36 Gianni Oliva, p.205.
37 Gianremo Armeni, *La strategia vincente del generale dalla Chiesa contro le Brigate Rosse... e la mafia* (Edizioni Associate, 2004), p.104.
38 Marco Clementi, p.98.
39 Ralf Steenbeek, 'De bestrijding van de Rode Brigades in Italië, 1974-1975. De methode van generaal Carlo Alberto Dalla Chiesa', *Leidschrift*, 23:1 (April 2008), p.117.
40 Roberto Bartali, 'Il PCI e le Brigate Rosse', in Salvatore Sechi, Le vene aperte del delitto Moro. Terrorismo, PCI, trame et servizi segreti (Polistampa, 2009), p.92.
41 Mario Moretti, p.127.
42 Marco Clementi, p.98.
43 Relazione della Commissione parlamentare d'inchiesta sulla strage di via Fani, sul sequestro e l'assassinio di Aldo Moro e sul terrorismo in Italia, vol. 4, Carlo Alberto Dalla Chiesa, 8 juli 1980, p.291.
44 Mario Moretti, pp.128–129.
45 Marcelle Padovani, p.148.
46 Commissione parlamentare d'inchiesta sul terrorismo in Italia e sulle cause della mancata individuazione dei responsabili delle stragi, Doc XXIII, n. 64, volume primo, Tomo 6, 2001, p.161.
47 Mario Moretti, pp.130–131.
48 Alberto Franceschini, p.238.
49 Commissione parlamentare d'inchiesta sul terrorismo in Italia e sulle cause della mancata individuazione dei responsabili delle stragi, Doc XXIII, n. 64, volume primo, Tomo 6, 2001, p.159.
50 Marco Clementi, p.108.
51 Turin prosecutor's office was also pressuring Dalla Chiesa to arrest Curcio swiftly for fear of losing him, Ralf Steenbeek, p.118.
52 Gianni Oliva, p.177.
53 Marco Clementi, p.112.
54 Prospero Gallinari, p.118.
55 Relazione della Commissione parlamentare d'inchiesta sulla strage di via Fani, sul sequestro e l'assassinio di Aldo Moro e sul terrorismo in Italia, vol. 4, Santillo, 8 juli 1980, p.476.
56 Giorgio Galli, p.65.
57 Marco Clementi, pp.116–117.
58 http://www.bibliotecamarxista.org/brigate%20rosse/1975/ds%2075.htm
59 Marco Clementi, p.120.
60 Mario Moretti, p.137.

61 Relazione della Commissione parlamentare d'inchiesta sulla strage di via Fani, sul sequestro e l'assassinio di Aldo Moro e sul terrorismo in Italia, vol. 4, Carlo Alberto Dalla Chiesa, 8 juli 1980, p.303.
62 Gianni Oliva, p.179.
63 Giorgio Galli, p.70.
64 Marco Clementi, p.127.
65 Gianni Oliva, p.180.
66 Gianni Oliva, p.180.
67 Marco Clementi, p.128.
68 Marco Clementi, p.129.
69 Giorgio Galli, p.72.
70 Giorgio Galli, p.79.
71 Ralf Steenbeek, p.121.
72 Giorgio Galli, p.79.

Chapter 5

1 Marco Clementi, pp.130–131.
2 Giorgio Galli, p.81.
3 Commissione parlamentare di inchiesta sul rapimento e sulla morte di Aldo Moro, Doc XXIII, N. 29, 2017, p.53.
4 Marco Clementi, p.133.
5 Chiara Dogliotti, p.83.
6 Chiara Dogliotti, p.90.
7 Gianni Oliva, p.214.
8 Mario Moretti, p.145.
9 Marco Clementi, p.141.
10 Marco Clementi, p.142.
11 Marco Clementi, p.143.
12 Commissione parlamentare d'inchiesta sul terrorismo in Italia e sulle cause della mancata individuazione dei responsabili delle stragi, Doc XXIII, n. 64, volume primo, Tomo 6, 2001, p.159.
13 Commissione parlamentare di inchiesta sul rapimento e sulla morte di Aldo Moro, Doc XXIII, N. 29, 2017, p.17.
14 Marco Clementi, p.144.
15 The accused were Pietro Bassi, Pietro Bertolazzi, Alfredo Bonavita, Renato Curcio, Valerio De Ponti, Paolo Maurizio Ferrari, Alberto Franceschini, Prospero Gallinari, Arialdo Lintrami, Roberto Ognibene and Tonino Paroli.
16 Prospero Gallinari, p.132.
17 Gianni Oliva, p.218.
18 Mario Moretti, p.159.
19 Chiara Dogliotti, pp.75–76.
20 Marco Clementi, p.152.
21 Mario Moretti, pp.175–176.
22 Domenico Guzzo, p.657.
23 Mario Moretti, p.144.
24 Marco Clementi, p.156.
25 Domenico Guzzo, p.653.
26 Domenico Guzzo, p.477.
27 Nanni Balestrini & Primo Moroni, pp.511–515.
28 Domenico Guzzo, pp.484–485.
29 Gianni Oliva, p.222.
30 Gianni Oliva, p.223.
31 Giorgio Galli, pp.99–100.
32 Isabelle Sommier, p.102.
33 Mario Moretti, pp.169–171.
34 Domenico Guzzo, p.490.
35 Domenico Guzzo, p.612.
36 Gianni Oliva, pp.223–225.
37 Sue Ellen Moran (ed.), *Courts Depositions of Three Red Brigadists* (DTIC, February 1986), pp.43–45.
38 Giorgio Galli, p.102.
39 Guillaume Guidon, *Images de la violence, violence des images. La violence politique et sa représentation dans la photographie de presse italienne (1969-1984)* (Université de Grenoble-Alpes, 2010), p.55.
40 Domenico Guzzo, p.655.
41 Sue Ellen Moran (ed.), p.46.
42 Chiara Dogliotti, p.95.
43 SIP was the Italian telephone company.
44 Domenico Guzzo, p.658.
45 Gianni Oliva, pp.230–231.
46 Prospero Gallinari, p.158.
47 Sue Ellen Moran (ed.), p.42.
48 Marco Clementi, p.186.
49 Alessandro Orsini, *Anatomia delle Brigate Rosse* (Rubbettino, 2010), p.99.
50 Mario Moretti, p.179.
51 Franco Bonisoli, a member of the BR executive committee, says it was in 1976 that the idea for the Moro kidnapping was born, Philippe Foro, *Une longue saison de douleur et de mort* (Vendémiaire, 2011), p.134.
52 Marco Clementi, p.195.
53 Philippe Foro, pp.136–137.
54 Giorgio Galli, p.95.
55 Vincenzo Marini Recchia & Giuseppe Zupo, *Operazione Moro* (Franco Angeli Editore, 1984), p.280.
56 Gianni Oliva, p.259.
57 Giorgio Galli, p.112.
58 Gianni Oliva, p.260.
59 Prospero Gallinari, p.182.
60 Mario Moretti, p.213.

Chapter 6

1 Unlike Prospero Gallinaro, Moretti says the choice of the date for Moro's kidnapping was linked to logistical constraints and not to the political importance of that day, Mario Moretti, p.182.
2 Philippe Foro, p.8.
3 Romano Bianco & Manlio Castronuovo, *Via Fani ore 9.02* (Nutrimenti, 2010), p.10.
4 All four tyres of the florist's car were punctured to prevent him from arriving at his place of work at the usual time.
5 Mario Moretti, p.188.
6 Romano Bianco & Manlio Castronuovo, p.11.
7 Barbara Balzerani, *Camarade Lune* (Cambourakis, 2017), p.76.
8 Mario Moretti, p.187.
9 Mario Moretti, pp.194–195.
10 Romano Bianco & Manlio Castronuovo, p.13.
11 Philippe Foro, pp.192–193.
12 Philippe Foro, pp.139–141.
13 According to the communist senator, Sergio Flamigni, the BR would have used several hiding places which the latter have always denied, Philippe Foro, p.78.
14 Philippe Foro, p.79.
15 Philippe Foro, p.82.
16 Commissione parlamentare d'inchiesta sul terrorismo in Italia e sulle cause della mancata individuazione dei responsabili delle stragi, Doc XXIII, n. 64, volume primo, Tomo 1, 2001, p.24.
17 Mario Moretti, p.205.
18 Philippe Foro, pp.68–72.
19 http://www.bibliotecamarxista.org/brigate%20rosse/1978/br%20moro%201.htm
20 Commissione parlamentare d'inchiesta sulla strage di via Fani, sul sequestro e l'assassinio di Aldo Moro e sul terrorismo in Italia, Doc XXIII, n. 5, Vol. 1, 1983, p.35.
21 Gianni Oliva, p.269.
22 Philippe Foro, pp.142–145.
23 http://www.bibliotecamarxista.org/brigate%20rosse/1978/br%20moro%203.htm
24 Philippe Foro, pp.91–92.
25 Philippe Foro, p.153. Rather, this spiritualism session would be a subterfuge allowing Prodi to protect the sources he possessed, especially in the circles of the extra-parliamentary left at the Bologna University where he taught.
26 Commissione parlamentare d'inchiesta sul terrorismo in Italia e sulle cause della mancata individuazione dei responsabili delle stragi, Doc XXIII, n. 64, volume primo, Tomo 6, 2001, p.215.
27 http://www.bibliotecamarxista.org/brigate%20rosse/1978/br%20moro%206.htm
28 Marcelle Padovani, p.123.
29 Commissione parlamentare d'inchiesta sul terrorismo in Italia e sulle cause della mancata individuazione dei responsabili delle stragi, Doc XXIII, n. 64, volume primo, Tomo 6, 2001, p.215.
30 Commissione parlamentare d'inchiesta sul terrorismo in Italia e sulle cause della mancata individuazione dei responsabili delle stragi, Doc XXIII, n. 64, volume primo, Tomo 6, 2001, p.212.
31 http://www.bibliotecamarxista.org/brigate%20rosse/1978/br%20moro%20falso%207.htm
32 According to Steve Pieczenik, the false Communication came from Interior Ministry officials who sought to test the reaction of the

population to the news of Moro's death while preparing them for the event, Philippe Foro, pp.103–104.
33 Philippe Foro, p.103.
34 Philippe Foro, p.113.
35 http://www.bibliotecamarxista.org/brigate%20rosse/1978/br%20moro%208.htm
36 Philippe Foro, p.108.
37 Gianni Oliva, pp.296–297.
38 Philippe Foro, p.109.
39 Philippe Foro, p.123.
40 Gianni Oliva, pp.300–301.
41 Philippe Foro, p.152.
42 Commissione parlamentare d'inchiesta sul terrorismo in Italia e sulle cause della mancata individuazione dei responsabili delle stragi, Doc XXIII, n. 64, volume primo, Tomo 6, 2001, p.210.
43 Philippe Foro, pp.154–155.
44 Commissione parlamentare d'inchiesta sul terrorismo in Italia e sulle cause della mancata individuazione dei responsabili delle stragi, Doc XXIII, n.64, volume primo, tomo 6, 2001, p.188.
45 Gianni Oliva, pp.307–308.
46 Commissione parlamentare d'inchiesta sulla strage di via Fani, sul sequestro e l'assassinio di Aldo Moro e sul terrorismo italiano, Doc XXIII, n. 5, Vol. 4, 1984, pp.194–195.
47 Luciana Stortoni, p.223.
48 Gianni Oliva, p.306.
49 Philippe Foro, p.182.
50 Alberto Franceschini, p.128.
51 https://tempspresents.com/category/hyperion/
52 Gianni Oliva, pp.308–309.
53 Commissione parlamentare d'inchiesta sul terrorismo in Italia e sulle cause della mancata individuazione dei responsabili delle stragi, Doc XXIII, n. 64, volume primo, Tomo 1, 2001, p.23.
54 Philippe Foro, pp.192–195.

Chapter 7

1 Giorgio Galli, p.133.
2 Sue Ellen Moran (ed.), p.41.
3 Mario Moretti, pp.273–274.
4 Mario Moretti, p.273.
5 Sue Ellen Moran (ed.), p.43.
6 Commissione parlamentare d'inchiesta sulla strage di via Fani, sul sequestro e l'assassinio di Aldo Moro e sul terrorismo italiano, Doc XXIII, n. 5, Vol. 1, 1983, p.57.
7 Chiara Dogliotti, p.105.
8 Mario Moretti, p.273.
9 Giorgio Galli, p.138.
10 Sue Ellen Moran (ed.), p.40.
11 Domenico Guzzo, p.677.
12 Marcelle Padovani, p.213.
13 Commissione parlamentare d'inchiesta sulla strage di via Fani, sul sequestro e l'assassinio di Aldo Moro e sul terrorismo italiano, Doc XXIII, n. 5, Vol. 4, 1984, p.244.
14 Marco Clementi, p.226.
15 Commissione parlamentare d'inchiesta sul terrorismo in Italia e sulle cause della mancata individuazione dei responsabili delle stragi, Doc XXIII, n. 64, volume primo, Tomo 6, 2001, p.184.
16 Philippe Foro, pp.156–157.
17 Commissione parlamentare d'inchiesta sul terrorismo in Italia e sulle cause della mancata individuazione dei responsabili delle stragi, Doc XXIII, n. 64, volume primo, Tomo 1, 2001, pp.55–57.
18 Marco Clementi, p.226.
19 Marco Clementi, p.47. The hiding place on Via Monte Nevoso was not discovered until 1990 during flat renovations.
20 Mario Moretti, p.283.
21 Enrico Fenzi, *Armes & bagages. Journal des Brigades Rouges* (Les Belles Lettres, 2008), pp.89–101
22 Giorgio Galli, p.157.
23 Chiara Dogliotti, pp.107–109.
24 Mario Moretti, p.275.
25 Chiara Dogliotti, p.112.
26 Todd H. DeGhetto, *Precipitating the Decline of Terrorist Groups: A Systems Analysis* (Naval Postgraduate School, 1994), p.61.
27 Marco Clementi, p.233.
28 Chiara Dogliotti, pp.100–121.
29 Mario Moretti, p.282.
30 Marco Clementi, p.235.
31 Prospero Gallinari, pp.211–212.
32 Marco Clementi, p.237.
33 Domenico Guzzo, pp.694–695.
34 Domenico Guzzo, p.677.
35 Marco Clementi, p.238.
36 Mario Moretti, pp.285–286.
37 Marco Clementi, p.238.
38 Prospero Gallinari, p.218.
39 Commissione parlamentare di inchiesta sul rapimento e sulla morte di Aldo Moro, Doc XXIII, N. 29, 2017, p.38.
40 Mario Moretti, p.287.
41 Marco Clementi, p.239.
42 Enrico Fenzi, p.167.
43 Sue Ellen Moran (ed.), p.17.
44 Mario Moretti pp.290–291.
45 Sue Ellen Moran (ed.), p.189.
46 Marco Clementi, p.241.
47 Chiara Dogliotti, p.254.
48 Domenico Guzzo, p.698.
49 Giorgio Galli, p.157.
50 Marco Clementi, p.246.
51 Marco Clementi, p.248.
52 Chiara Dogliotti, p.122.
53 Marco Clementi, p.247.
54 Gianni Oliva, p.326.
55 Giorgio Galli, p.162.
56 Mario Moretti, p.296.
57 Commissione parlamentare d'inchiesta sulla strage di via Fani, sul sequestro e l'assassinio di Aldo Moro e sul terrorismo italiano, Doc XXIII, n. 5, Vol. 4, 1984, p.256–257.
58 Marco Clementi, p.251.
59 Giorgio Galli, p.164.
60 US Senate, 'Terrorism and Security: The Italian Experience', Report of the Subcommittee on Security and Terrorism of the Committee on the Judiciary United States Senate, November 1984, p.16.
61 US Senate, 'Terrorism and Security: The Italian Experience', p.6.
62 Chiara Dogliotti, p.202.
63 Chiara Dogliotti, pp.133–135.
64 Commissione parlamentare d'inchiesta sulla strage di via Fani, sul sequestro e l'assassinio di Aldo Moro e sul terrorismo italiano, Doc XXIII, n. 5, Vol. 4, 1984, p.76.
65 Sue Ellen Moran (ed.), pp.197–210.
66 Enrico Fenzi, p.198
67 Marco Clementi, p.270.
68 Sue Ellen Moran (ed.), p.211.
69 Mario Moretti, p.301.
70 Enrico Fenzi, p.222.
71 https://www.albadeifuneralidiunostato.org/1980/12/
72 Mario Moretti, p.305.
73 Giorgio Galli, p.172.
74 Marco Clementi, p.277.
75 Giorgio Galli, p.172.
76 Mario Moretti, p.306.
77 Marco Clementi, pp.279–285.
78 Mario Moretti, pp.313–314.

Chapter 8

1 Mario Moretti, p.140.
2 Chiara Dogliotti, pp.26–27.
3 Chiara Dogliotti, p.25.
4 Chiara Dogliotti, p.38.
5 Sue Ellen Moran (ed.), p.208.
6 Stefano Quirico, 'Il modello organizzativo delle Brigate rosse in una prospettiva comparata', pp.61–88.
7 Chiara Dogliotti, p.35.
8 Chiara Dogliotti, pp.137–141.
9 Risoluzione della Direzione Strategica no. 2, <http://www.bibliotecamarxista.org/brigate%20rosse/1974/ds2.htm>
10 *Norme di comportamento*, <http://www.bibliotecamarxista.org/brigate%20rosse/1974/norme%20comp%20parz.htm>
11 Marcelle Padovani, pp.39–40.
12 This amount is equivalent to around 600 euros today.

13 Marcelle Padovani, pp.44–45.
14 Marcelle Padovani, p.37.
15 Sue Ellen Moran (ed.), p.10.
16 Alberto Franceschini, p.139.
17 Mario Moretti, p.140.
18 Philippe Foro, p.27.
19 Sue Ellen Moran (ed.), p.26.
20 Mario Moretti, p.176.
21 Marcelle Padovani, p.207.
22 To this figure can be added 113 arrests for the BR-Walter Alasia, 147 for the BR-PG, 93 for the BR-PCC and 73 for the BR-UCC.
23 Mario Moretti, p.272.
24 Commissione parlamentare d'inchiesta sul terrorismo in Italia e sulle cause della mancata individuazione dei responsabili delle stragi, Doc XXIII, n. 64, volume primo, Tomo 1, 2001, p.67.
25 'Terrorism and Security: The Italian Experience', p.20.
26 Marcelle Padovani, p.131.
27 Christian Jansen, 'Brigate Rosse und Rote Armee Fraktion. ProtagonistInnen, Propaganda und Praxis des Terrorismus der frühen siebziger Jahre', in Oliver von Mengersen et al., Personen – Soziale Bewegungen – Parteien. Beiträge zur Neuesten Geschichte. Festschrift für Hartmut Soell (Manutius, 2004), p.491.
28 Commissione parlamentare d'inchiesta sulla strage di via Fani, sul sequestro e l'assassinio di Aldo Moro e sul terrorismo italiano, Doc XXIII, n. 5, Vol. 1, 1983, p.130.
29 Mario Moretti, pp.262–266.
30 Alberto Franceschini, p.92.
31 Marcelle Padovani, p.134.
32 Michael Ploetz, 'Mit RAF, Roten Brigaden und Action Directe Terrorismus und Rechtsextremismus in der Strategie von SED und KPdSU', *Zeitschrift des Forschungsverbundes SED-Staat*, 22 (2007), pp.134–135.
33 Gianluca, Falanga, *Spie dall'est. L'Italia nelle carte segrete della Stasi* (Caroci, 2014).
34 Marco Bruni, *Il caso Moro negli atti del Ministero per la sicurezza di Stato della Repubblica Democratica Tedesca* (Sapienza Università di Roma, 2015), p.123.
35 Marco Bruni, p.138.
36 Commissione parlamentare d'inchiesta sul terrorismo in Italia e sulle cause della mancata individuazione dei responsabili delle stragi, Doc XXIII, n. 64, volume primo, Tomo 1, 2001, p.34.
37 Roberto Bartali, 'Il PCI e le Brigate Rosse', p.109.
38 Fernando Orlandi, 'A Praga, a Praga!' in Salvatore Sechi, Le vene aperte del delitto Moro. Terrorismo, PCI, trame et servizi segreti (Polostampa, 2009) pp.119–161.
39 Marco Bruni, p.133.
40 Fernando Orlandi, 'La prima volta del KGB sulle Brigate rosse', in *East Europe and Asia Strategies*, no. 34 (February 2011), pp.25–26.
41 Mario Moretti, p.268.
42 After the splits that would soon destroy the BR unit, the IRA warehouse was dismantled; in particular, the BR-Guerilla Party appropriated the weapons (a pair of bazookas, explosives, and surface-to-air missiles), which were later found by police during arrests in the early 1980s.
43 Gianni Oliva, p.352.
44 Luca Falciola, 'Transnational Relationships between the Italian Revolutionary Left and Palestinian Militants during the Cold War', *Journal of Cold War Studies*, 22:4 (Fall 2020), pp.31–70.
45 Marcelle Padovani, p.49.
46 Chiara Dogliotti, p.86.
47 Mario Moretti, pp.184–185.
48 Prospero Gallinari, p.183.
49 Nanni Balestrini & Primo Moroni, p.382.
50 Mario Moretti, p.187.
51 Relazione della Commissione parlamentare d'inchiesta sulla strage di via Fani, sul sequestro e l'assassinio di Aldo Moro e sul terrorismo in Italia, vol. 4, pp.387–388.
52 Chiara Dogliotti, p.100.
53 Mario Moretti, p.113.
54 Commissione parlamentare d'inchiesta sulla strage di via Fani, sul sequestro e l'assassinio di Aldo Moro e sul terrorismo italiano, Doc XXIII, n. 5, Vol. 4, 1984, p.71.
55 Commissione parlamentare d'inchiesta sulla strage di via Fani, sul sequestro e l'assassinio di Aldo Moro e sul terrorismo italiano, Doc XXIII, n. 5, Vol. 4, 1984, p.133.
56 Mario Moretti, pp.268–270.
57 Marcelle Padovani, p.135.
58 Mario Moretti, p.194.
59 Sue Ellen Moran (ed.), p.85. Editorial note: the above is verbatim as per the quoted source. It seems likely that the items actually being described include an AKM assault rifle and a 9mm Browning HP pistol with magazine.
60 Chiara Dogliotti, p.87.
61 Mario Moretti, pp.151–152.
62 Mario Moretti, pp.167–168.
63 *Notes et études de l'Institut de criminologie de Paris*, no. 3, décembre 1987.

Chapter 9

1 Sue Ellen Moran (ed.), p.226.
2 Chiara Dogliotti, p.277.
3 Chiara Dogliotti, p.265.
4 Marco Clementi, p.293.
5 Marco Clementi, p.294.
6 Chiara Dogliotti, p.279–294.
7 Marco Clementi, p.296.
8 Chiara Dogliotti, p.203.
9 Marco Clementi, pp.297–299.
10 Marco Clementi, p.300.
11 Giorgio Galli, p.186.
12 Domenico Guzzo, p.717.
13 Gianni Oliva, p.333.
14 Giorgio Galli, p.197.
15 Giorgio Galli, p.188.
16 Marcelle Padovani, p.211.
17 https://www.ugomariatassinari.it/speciale-sequestro-dozier-1/
18 Chiara Dogliotti, p.209.
19 Larry Allen Buckingham, *The Red Brigades: A description of a Terrorist Organization* (California State University, 1982), p.50.
20 Jeffrey T. Richelson, '"Truth Conquers All Chains": The U.S. Army Intelligence Support Activity, 1981-1989', *International Journal of Intelligence and CounterIntelligence*, 12:2 (1999), pp.168–200.
21 https://www.ugomariatassinari.it/generale-dozier/
22 Gianni Oliva, p.336.
23 Luciana Stortoni, p.249.
24 Luciana Stortoni, p.245.
25 Marco Clementi, p.321.
26 Marco Clementi, p.322.
27 http://www.bibliotecamarxista.org/brigate%20rosse/1982/volanitno%20ritirata%20strategica.htm
28 Marco Clementi, p.315.
29 Domenico Guzzo, p.718.
30 Mario Moretti, p.340.
31 Giorgio Galli, p.194.
32 Chiara Dogliotti, pp.267–270.
33 Giorgio Galli, p.204.
34 Chiara Dogliotti, p.272.
35 Marco Clementi, p.326.
36 Marco Clementi, p.331.
37 Commissione parlamentare d'inchiesta sulla strage di via Fani sul sequestro e l'assassinio di Aldo Moro e sul terrorismo in Italia, Doc. XXIII, n. 5, vol. 91, p.134.
38 https://www.cremonaoggi.it/2018/01/31/31-gennaio-1983-35-anni-brusco-risveglio-cremona-col-covo-delle-br-via-volturno/
39 Giorgio Galli, p.203.
40 Marco Clementi, p.324.
41 Gianni Oliva, p.337.
42 Marco Clementi, p.335.
43 Giorgio Galli, p.219.
44 Gianni Oliva, p.337.
45 Domenico Di Petrillo, *Il lungo assedio. La lotta al terrorismo nel diario operativo della Sezione Speciale Anticrimine Carabinieri di Roma* (Melampo, 2018), p.231.
46 Domenico Di Petrillo, *Il lungo assedio*, pp.212–226.
47 Marco Clementi, p.349.
48 Giorgio Galli, p.225.
49 Gianni Oliva, p.338.

Continued on page 76

ACKNOWLEDGEMENTS

This book would not have been written without the support, encouragement and help of all the Helion Publishing team. I would like to thank especially Tom Cooper and Andy Miles who came up with the idea for this book. I want to thank them for the idea, but also for their patience and benevolence towards me.

I also thank Albert Grandolini for his kindness in sharing the photos from his collection.

To finish, I want to devote this book to my grandfather, who died a few years ago, and who was born in Villa Sant'Angelo, a small Italian village in the province of Abruzzo.

ABOUT THE AUTHOR

David Francois, from France, earned his PhD in Contemporary History at the University of Burgundy and specialised in studying militant communism, its military history and the relationship between politics and violence in contemporary history. In 2009, he co-authored the *Guide des archives de l'Internationale communiste* published by the French National Archives and the Maison des sciences de l'Homme in Dijon. He regularly contributes articles for various French military history magazines and is a regular contributor to the French history website L'autre côté de la colline.

Continued from page 75

50 https://siulp.it/roma-14-febbraio-1987-assalto-di-via-prati-di-papa/
51 Domenico Di Petrillo, p.236.
52 Domenico Di Petrillo, p.354.
53 Mario Moretti, p.345.
54 Marco Clementi, pp.361–366.
55 Gianni Oliva, p.338.
56 http://www.bibliotecamarxista.org/brigate%20rosse/1988/testo%20raf%20br.htm
57 Stéphane Joahny, 'Quand Paris servait de base arrière aux Brigades rouges', *Le Journal du dimanche* (14 July 2018).
58 Gianni Oliva, p.339.
59 Many reasons have been given to explain Mitterrand's leniency: the desire not to make France a rear base for the Italian armed struggle, the idea that the Italian refugees belonged to the 'Family Album' of the left-wing but also the memory of the hospitality of the Italian authorities towards the fugitives of the Organisation armée secréte, the terrorist formation of the French Algeria partisans which spilled blood in France in the early 1960s.
60 Stéphane Joahny, *Le Journal du dimanche* (14 July 2018).
61 Maurizio Di Marzio managed to escape.